NEEDLEWORK

TIPS

for the

NOVICE and EXPERT

SANDY RODGERS

A MANUAL OF PROVEN METHODS

TO

IMPROVE YOUR NEEDLEWORK

First Printing November, 1995
Second Printing July, 1996

Also by Sandy Rodgers:

SILK AND METAL THREADS ON CANVAS

THE ART OF TEACHING EMBROIDERY

The Yarn Cellar Publishing Company
720 Shaker Drive
Medina, Ohio 44256-2660

TABLE OF CONTENTS

ACKNOWLEDGEMENTS

No book is written without the help of many people. I would like to extend my thanks to :

He, who has given us all talent.

Dave, my partner in all aspects of life.

Karlene and Bob, Mary and Jim, Sarah and Timothy, who give so much joy to life.

Karlene Weiss, Joan Masterson, Kaye Neufeld, and Carlene Harwick, who have once again shared their knowledge and expertise by editing for me.

Karen Conley and Jill Rabius-McGrath, for supplementing my information on quilting and beading needles.

This book is dedicated to all those who enhance the beauty of our world by means of a needle and thread. I hope that your needlework will be improved with the use of the suggestions that follow.

Thank you.

INTRODUCTION

This book contains no exquisite needlework patterns and no diagrams of beautiful stitches. It is, however, full of ideas to make that pattern even more exquisite and the stitches even more beautiful.

Needlework Tips for the Novice and Expert evolved from a request of the Embroiderers' Guild of America, Inc., to make suggestions for new stitchers. I was asked to list things we learn through experience. As I sat at the computer to fulfill that assignment, I found that before I finished typing one topic, another popped into mind. I was finally forced to stop by the set page limits. The resounding success of that EGA publication and requests of many students to expand the concept, caused me to gather years of notes and greatly increase that first venture. I found that the hardest part of writing this book was to force myself to stop. Other than that, this has been the easiest of my books to write. There seemed to be no end to items I wanted to include.

Suggestions and ideas in this book have come from many sources. From teachers in whose classes I have been privileged to study; from my own students, across the United States and in many other countries, who sometimes gave me a solution, and sometimes presented a problem asking me to develop the answer; and from casual conversations with fellow stitchers while relaxing after class at a seminar.

It is impossible to include a bibliography in *Needlework Tips for the Novice and Expert* because most items reflect methods I use regularly when I stitch. They are things I know from experience and years of doing needlework, with no knowledge of how or when I learned them. Some were ideas I jotted on a scrap of paper and stuck in a folder for future use. At the time, I had no plan of how to use

them, I only wanted to remember a solution in case I ever faced a similar problem. I have no memory from where these nuggets came.

Neither the author nor the publisher accept any responsibility for the results obtained by using the suggestions in this book. They are just that, suggestions, and should be used at the discretion of the reader. No guarantee is made for any of these recommendations. I have tried to give more than one solution or recommendation for every circumstance discussed.

The material is loosely grouped into sections as listed in the Table of Contents. I have tried to organize entries by subject within each of these sections. This was not always possible, since many items fall under more than one general topic. An effort has been made to achieve a logical order. Unfortunately, not all people think with the same form of logic.

When a specific suggestion is appropriate to more than one section, it may be presented in both. If you think you have read something before in this book, you may be right. A few items are of sufficient importance to repeat in each place where they are appropriate.

If you come across a term whose meaning you do not know, try looking it up in the index. The index is unusually detailed for just this reason. It is likely that the term in question will be listed there, and you will be directed to an entry which will help you.

Words such as "usually" and "generally" are used very often. This is because there are few absolutes in the world of needlework. Words similar to "always" and "never" must be used very sparingly.

As I write the last few words of this book, I find I already have several notes concerning ideas for which there simply is no more room. It appears that a sequel to *Needlework Tips for the Novice and Expert* is inevitable.

GROUND MATERIALS

◆ <u>GROUND</u> <u>MATERIAL</u>, or ground fabric, is anything you embellish with stitching. It may be fine lawn linen, metal window screening, lustrous satin, cotton, leather, burlap, canvas, or hundreds of other foundations.

◆ A *doodle cloth* is a scrap of the same ground fabric on which you are going to stitch your project. It is treated just as the project is, either placed in a hoop or mounted on a working frame. This is a practice piece, the place to test stitches and threads.

When a doodle cloth is full of practice work, it can be cut into small sections with one experiment on each. These may then be placed in a notebook for future reference. Or, do the doodles so that they form a small design. Then you will have a practice piece and a completed project at once. The first samplers were a form of practice. They were actually doodle cloths.

◆ It really does make a difference whether you stitch on the right or wrong side of linen. Generally the difference is in appearance, but some experts say it is easier to stitch on the 'right' side. To find the right side, hold fabric by diagonally opposite corners. Pull slightly on the bias. The linen fabric will curl toward the right side.

◆ If the ground material is mounted on a working frame, protect stitched areas of your embroidery with a piece of fabric. Place this fabric over completed sections. It will keep your hands and arms from rubbing the stitching and causing the thread to 'pill.' It will also protect those areas from becoming soiled. Consider covering areas not yet worked. Covering unstitched sections can help avoid snagging the thread if your ground material has a sizing which causes it to be stiff, as does most canvas. Some people like to cut a hole in the center of their cloth to

expose only the section being stitched — all other areas are covered.

A piece of washed cotton muslin works well for your cover cloth. A blend such as polyester-cotton may be used for a cover cloth provided you do not object to having synthetics in contact with your needlework. Those who are concerned with conservation will prefer a natural fabric of either cotton or linen. Many embroiderers like to use a man's washed handkerchief as a cover cloth.

The size depends on the size of your needlework, but 8" x 8" is generally sufficient for most projects. If you have a cover cloth of 10" x 10" you can cut a hole in the center so that only the area being worked is exposed. All other sections of the piece are protected.

◆   Carefully consider the color of your ground fabric in relation to the color of the threads. If the background is open and not covered with stitching, as in crewel, silk embroidery, or some canvas designs, that area will be the color of the ground fabric. Many stitchers take advantage of colored ground material and plan to leave it exposed in the background area. The color of the unstitched sections will interact with all threads in the piece. Be certain that the ground color enhances the design.

Even if the ground is covered with stitching, it can influence the color of the stitches. A white stitch on cream ground will appear whiter than a stitch of white on black fabric. Blue ground fabric can cause yellow stitches to look green.

◆   The color of the ground fabric is important if you are doing exposed canvas stitches in needlepoint. These stitches, or stitch patterns, allow the canvas to show through the worked threads — on purpose. The blending of the thread and ground color can produce a third color, which may not be the one you want.

◆   The above principle is also true if your are doing exposed fabric

stitches on a closely woven material. For example, open crewel stitches on linen will establish an interaction between thread and fabric colors.

◆ When doing needlepoint on white canvas, consider coloring the ground in the area that will be stitched with dark threads. Coloring the white canvas before doing sections of dark stitching will help eliminate flecks of white showing through the dark thread. 'Grin-through' is one of the names given to the unsightly condition of these white flecks. It is also called 'lice.'

Use acrylic paints or permanent markers in colors close to those of your threads. Be sure to test paints and markers on a scrap of fabric. Wet the tests to check that they will be colorfast. Even if you do not plan to dampen the needlework in any way, high humidly can cause non-fast paints and markers to bleed.

◆ If your entire design is to be worked in threads which are fairly dark, consider using a canvas other than white. Just about every size canvas comes in tan or brown, as well as white. One of these darker valued grounds may eliminate, or minimize, grin-through.

◆ To determine how many stitches there will be on a piece of evenweave fabric, including needlepoint canvas, count the number of threads in a linear, or running, inch. To assure that you have the correct number, take the count at three or four places, measuring some each vertically and horizontally on the material. Be sure that no measurement is within one-inch of the selvage. The weaving close to the selvage can be slightly tighter or looser than that in the rest of the material.

Your count of ground fabric threads in one inch will be the number of stitches per inch, assuming each stitch is over one intersection of vertical and horizonal threads. Do be careful to make adjustments if you are going to stitch over more than one intersection. Be aware that there may be a slight difference in the vertical and horizontal thread counts. This variation will seldom cause a problem.

♦ When considering needlepoint canvas, remember that a *mesh* is the intersection created by the crossing of a vertical and a horizontal thread. Canvas threads are just that, threads. They are not mesh. Only the place where two threads cross, a vertical and a horizontal, is a mesh.

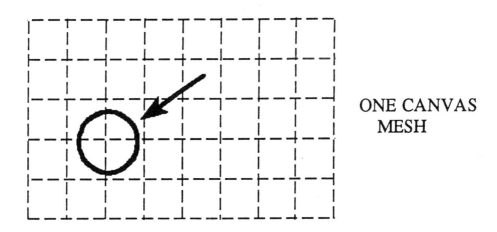

ONE CANVAS
MESH

♦ It is correct to state that a specific canvas has a given number *threads per inch*. It is also correct to say that the canvas has a given number *mesh per inch*. Yet another way to express the canvas size is to say that it is *XX count*.

♦ <u>MONO</u> <u>CANVAS</u> is a basic tabby weave. That is, the threads are woven over one and under one. Another name for this weave is *plain weave*. If stitched with a tension that is too tight, the threads can be pulled out of position. Such flexibility is required when doing pulled work. Since the threads are not stabilized, the canvas will ravel if the cut edges are not bound or secured in some way.

Mono canvas is available in 6, 8, 10, 12, 13, 14, 17, 18, 22, and 32 threads per inch. It is usually white or brown, however some colored canvas is manufactured. The greatest number of colors seems to be in 18 mesh.

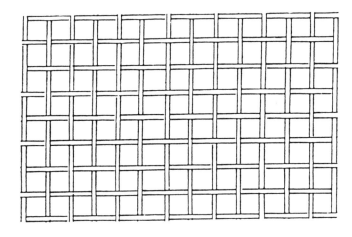

MONO CANVAS
ILLUSTRATING
TABBY WEAVE

◆ <u>CONGRESS</u> <u>CLOTH</u> is actually a fabric with an open, tabby weave. It is used as needlepoint canvas. Congress cloth is sometimes sold in 16 count, but most often found in 23 threads per inch.

To be totally correct, the mesh count of the smaller size congress cloth should be written as 23/24. All canvas has a slight irregularity of thread count somewhere in the bolt. In this case, the areas where the thread count varies between twenty-three and twenty-four threads per inch are more prevalent than with other canvas counts. The shift from twenty-three to twenty-four count will be gradual. Such a change would not be noticed on a single piece of ground fabric unless it is extremely large. In general usage, one of the two numbers is frequently dropped when describing congress cloth.

There is more than one manufacturer of congress cloth. Some are quite soft, others fairly stiff with sizing. Select the quality of congress cloth depending on the requirements of your project.

Congress cloth is woven in a rainbow of colors. Be careful of any water around this canvas, no matter what color it is. Some, but not all, brands of congress cloth will develop a permanent water spot where they are wet.

per inch. It is made in many colors, including gold and silver metallic, as well as clear.

Plastic canvas makes excellent stiffening lining for embroidered articles. However, care must be taken to only use it in washable items. Plastic canvas cannot be dry cleaned. The grid dissolves in the cleaning fluids.

◆ SILK GAUZE has an interlock construction, with threads made of silk. It is very fine, with counts of twenty-four to eighty-four threads per inch. This canvas has become very scarce and difficult to find. It is simply not being manufactured. In illustration of "supply and demand," the cost of silk gauze is several hundred dollars per yard.

A fairly new, polyester substitute for silk gauze is acceptable for many uses. It comes in eighteen, twenty-eight, and thirty threads per inch. The construction is the same as silk gauze, however polyester has a stiffer 'hand,' or feel, than the silk.

Both silk gauze, if it can be found, and the polyester gauze, are sold by the yard, or mounted in lightweight cardboard frames. If in a frame, stitching is to be done while the gauze is still so mounted. The cardboard frame serves as a working frame.

◆ WASTE CANVAS is thin canvas manufactured with so little sizing that it is almost flimsy. A piece should be basted to tightly woven fabric. Stitches are worked through the waste canvas and into the fabric, using the grid of the waste canvas as a guide. A commercial chart is usually followed for stitch and color placement. When the embroidery is finished, the waste canvas is dampened. What little sizing there is, will soften. Use tweezers to remove the canvas threads, leaving the stitched design on the fabric.

Since the canvas threads must be pulled out, it is wise to avoid complicated compound stitches. Tent or cross stitches usually work best on waste canvas.

Waste canvas generally has a blue thread woven every five or ten threads. Care should be taken not to mistake it for needlepoint canvas. It has little strength and will not support stitches without the addition of the tightly woven fabric.

◆ LINEN CANVAS Most canvas is made of cotton. Linen canvas is simply a mono, or single, weave material made of linen rather than cotton. It has a soft cream color and slight sheen which are very appealing. The threads are somewhat slippery and tend to shift easily. It is woven in counts which run from #13 to #50.

While linen canvas has a wonderful quality, it is much more expensive than cotton. Although some embroiderers are willing to pay extra for it, it is no longer in great demand because of the cost. Linen canvas is becoming very scarce.

◆ POLYESTER CANVAS In addition to the polyester canvas which has recently been introduced in place of silk gauze, there is a polyester that has been manufactured for some time. It is very flexible and soft, and is designed mainly to be used for garments. The weave is similar to an interlock. The polyester canvas is sometimes actually made of nylon, depending on manufacturer, and is usually available with 18 threads per inch.

◆ The strength and quality of cotton canvas is determined by the *denier*. Tiny strands are twisted together and covered with sizing to form a single canvas thread. The number of small components in each thread is the denier.

To check canvas denier, use your finger nail to remove the sizing from a single canvas thread. Untwist the thread. It will be easy to count the number of tiny strands in the bundle. A denier of five or six is excellent. Four is highly questionable as a good base for needlepoint, and fewer than four is definitely unacceptable.

◆ If you need to find the straight diagonal on a canvas, hold it at eye level. Adjust by turning slightly from one side to the other. It will be easy to see the diagonal channels. This is very helpful if you have a long diagonal row to stitch and want to check your accuracy.

◆ When cutting a piece of canvas ground fabric, be sure to add approximately 2" beyond the edges of the planned background, on each side. This is a total of 4" more lengthwise and 4" additional across the width. If the project is very large, the excess amount should be increased. This additional material around the edges of the embroidery will not be stitched. It will remain unworked and will be available for the finishing process. It can be folded over the mounting board if the project is a wall hanging, or it can be used as the selvages. This excess also provides the room to bind cut edges and to attach to a working frame.

◆ A design on soft ground fabric, such as linen, aida, or hardanger cloth, also requires additional excess, unworked fabric around the design area. Consider starting with 3" extra on each side. Adjust the additional amount of fabric in relation to the size of the piece.

◆ A canvas project which consists of several pieces should be worked on canvas which is all cut from the same bolt. There can be a slight difference in the count from one bolt to the next, even if they are woven to be the same. Thus, if you are working a vest with a front and back on #18 mesh, be sure that both pieces are stitched on canvas from the same bolt. Also, place both pieces in the same direction on the canvas. For example, the top-to-bottom measurement, vertical grain, should be positioned identically for the front and back. If the front is 'up and down,' on the canvas, and the back is placed 'sideways,' there could be an unplanned difference in the size of the two finished pieces. Canvas will frequently vary just slightly in the vertical and horizontal thread count.

zontally. Just think of the cartoon character Elmer Fudd, and his problem pronouncing words. Horizontal is right to left, or as Elmer would say "wright and weft."

◆ If doing a submission for an expertise testing program from one of the embroidery guilds, be sure to follow directions on selvage placement. Most programs require selvages on the left side.

◆ When storing extra pieces of canvas, try to lay them flat in a drawer. If they are too big for flat storage, roll them carefully into a tube. Then keep them placed horizontally. Do not stand the tube on end, if there is another option. If placed on its end, the edge of the canvas which bares the weight will squish. You may be able to get these wrinkles out by ironing, but it is better to avoid them entirely if at all possible.

◆ Needlepoint canvas that has creases can sometimes be rescued. The problem is caused by the sizing having been broken at the point of the crease. Press the canvas with a warm iron. Use the lowest heat setting that will give you steam. Keep moving the iron without allowing its weight to rest in one place. Permitting the iron to stay in one position too long will create a shiny, 'flattened,' surface on the canvas. The steam is what will do the work. Try holding the iron just above the canvas. You will get the steam without the weight of the iron. This steam will slightly soften the canvas sizing and straighten the fabric. When cool, the stiffening of the sizing will return.

◆ Other embroidery ground fabrics, such as linens for crewel or silk fabric, should be stored flat, if at all possible. Place it in a drawer to give extra protection from dust and dirt. For large pieces, use a cardboard tube. Cover the tube with washed muslin or acid-free tissue paper. Wrap the fabric around the tube and cover with another piece of muslin or tissue. It is important to avoid creases.

THREADS

◆ The words *thread(s)* and *fiber(s)* are not interchangeable. Fibers are very tiny pieces of natural material: cotton, linen, or wool. Many, many fibers are combined together to form a thread.

A thread is composed of fibers, however fibers are not made up of threads. Therefore, since the two words do not have the same meaning, they cannot be used interchangeably.

It is interesting to note that several of the large embroidery organizations have asked their teachers and members not to use the word 'fibers' when they mean 'threads.'

◆ Cotton, linen, wool, and silk are natural threads. Other threads are man-made or a combination of natural and man-made.

◆ A fiber is a very tiny piece of plant material. A filament was first a liquid which hardened. Silk, even though it is grouped with the natural threads, is actually composed of filaments, not fibers. Cotton, linen, and wool are fashioned from fibers.

◆ Yarn is generally accepted as having a fuzzy texture. Thread is usually thought of as being smooth.

◆ There are several important terms which are concerned with yarns and threads. Quotations in the following are from *A Dictionary of Textile Terms* by Dan River, Inc., 1992. It is a highly recommended list of terms for those interested in yarn and textiles, without being excessively technical. If you wish to order this booklet, please contact the company at: Dictionary Department, Dan River Inc., 111 W. 40th

Street, New York, NY 10018. Enclose a check for $2.00 made out to Dan River, Inc.

FIBER — "The fundamental unit comprising a textile raw material such as cotton, wool, etc." It is similar to an exceedingly fine, hair-like, strand.

FILAMENT — A strand, usually very thin, of acetate, rayon, nylon, or polyester, or "The single unit which is extruded by a silk-worm in spinning its cocoon." Generally a fiber is considered to be 'fuzzy,' a filament is smooth.

YARN — A somewhat fuzzy cord of spun or twisted fibers.

THREAD — A smooth cord, of various degrees of firmness, made from either fibers or filaments. It lacks the hairy characteristic of yarn.

PLY — Tiny fibers, or filaments, which have been tightly twisted together. For example, a commonly used thread in needlework is embroidery floss or stranded cotton. As it comes from the skein, the thread is composed of six smaller strands. When untwisted, it is easy to see that each small strand contains two plies. When one of the plies is untwisted, you can see that it is composed of fibers. The plural of ply is 'plies.'

SINGLE, or SINGLE YARN — "One that has not been plied; the result of drawing, twisting and winding a mass of fibers into a coherent yarn." A ply is composed of two or more singles.

BLEND — A yarn of two or more types of fibers or filaments which are twisted together. Most often these are natural and man-made combinations such as cotton and polyester. Currently there is a silk and wool blend thread available, two natural threads, but such combinations are not commonly sold for hand embroidery.

TWIST — The turning which holds fibers or filaments together to form plies or threads. Threads have one of two types of twist, S-twist or Z-twist. Identify which twist your thread has by comparing it to the spine, or central portion, of an S and a Z. Most threads designed for hand work have a S-twist. Generally threads created for machine work have a Z-twist. When stitching, right-handed people will find that Z-twist threads untwist more easily than do S-twists. The reverse is true for left-handed embroiderers.

◆ To remove an unwanted knot in a fine thread, such as one strand of stranded embroidery cotton, use two tapestry needles. Slip the blunt point of each needle, one at a time, through the loop formed by the knot. Then gently pull the needles against the sides of the loop. Repeat as often as necessary to release the knot.

The size of the tapestry needle depends on the thickness of the thread and how tight the knot. The thinner the thread and tighter the knot, the finer the needle. Usually #26 or #28 tapestry needles will work easiest. Using your fingernails or the points of sharp needles to untie knots can mar, or even shred, the thread.

◆ Take care of your threads — they are expensive. When storing before using, keep them from light, moisture, and dust. It is best to place them in a washed, muslin bag. Air may then circulate, but the threads are protected from dust. A washed pillow case is acceptable, too.

Delicate threads need to be placed in a rigid container so that they will not be crushed. Real metals should first be wrapped in acid free tissue paper. Your needlework shop probably carries this tissue, or they can get it for you.

Man-made threads do well in plastic bags as long as they are out of direct lighting and away from excessive heat.

Do not keep any thread in an air-tight container, or plastic bags that are tightly closed with a 'twister.' Also avoid zip type plastic bags. Trapped moisture can form mildew in even the driest climate.

Generally, keep the thread the way you purchased it. If it is on a reel or spool, wrapped on a card, or folded into a skein, it is usually best to store it that way until you are ready to use it.

◆ Thread manufacturers and importers say that food-quality plastic bags are good for thread storage, as long as you do not use 'twisters' or make the bag air tight. Place the threads inside and just fold under the open end. Do not use these bags for long term storage, such as a year or more. If you use clear food-quality plastic bags, be careful to keep them away from light. Since light will pass through them, the threads inside can fade.

◆ Generally, put the 'pull end' of the thread into the needle. That is, if you pull a piece of thread from a reel or spool, put that end in the needle, not the end where you cut the strand. It seems to cause fewer knots if threaded this way. It has to do with the way the thread is spun and wound on the spool. The same is true of both embroidery and regular sewing threads.

◆ Wool, cotton, and linen threads have a direction. The thread should be stitched through the ground so that the tiny fibers of which it is composed are smoothed down flat. This direction is further intensified by the spinning process. If the thread is pulled through the 'wrong' way, these fibers will be ruffled and tangled. To illustrate, if you pat and stroke a kitten from nose to tail, you will smooth her fur. If you stroke from tail to nose, you will ruffle the fur.

To find the direction of these threads, draw a piece between the fingers, or thumb and first finger, of your dominate hand. Then turn the thread end-for-end, and pull it between the same fingers again. One way will feel smoother than the other. This is *with* the direction.

Silk thread, because it is composed of filaments rather than fibers, has no direction. Any smooth/bumpy sensation felt on the thread is due only to the spinning process. It is totally impossible to stitch so that all filaments are smooth. The slight difference in direction caused by spinning will make no difference in the appearance of your embroidery.

Man-made threads, as of this writing, have no direction.

Many instructors and skilled needleartists feel that it is not necessary to be concerned about the direction of wool, cotton, or linen threads. Their conviction is that any difference in position of these tiny fibers will not affect the final appearance of the work. Each embroiderer must decide, individually, whether the direction of the thread is important.

◆ Basic types of wool yarn used for embroidery are *tapestry, crewel,* and *persian.* Each of these yarns is produced by more than one manufacturer.

TAPESTRY YARN is a tightly twisted thread, used as it comes from the manufacturer. It is not separated. It is durable and excellent for chair seats, rugs, and items which will receive hard wear. Since it does not separate well it must be used with needlepoint canvas that is the correct size for good coverage. If used for surface embroidery, it creates stitches with heavy texture.

CREWEL YARN is produced from two plies of wool, each fairly thin. They are loosely twisted together and can be easily separated. Because the full strand of crewel wool is not thick, and because it can be further divided, it is extremely versatile. The full strand can be combined with others to create the required coverage on various sizes of needlepoint canvas. Two or more plies, of different colors or values, can be joined to form another color or value. The same procedures can be applied to

separated strands. Unfortunately, the loose twist of crewel yarn also means that it does not wear well. Crewel yarn is well suited for both needlepoint and surface work, unless the item will receive hard wear.

PERSIAN YARN is composed of three plies, each with a medium twist. These plies are loosely combined, making them easy to separate. The individual plies can be separated and recombined as desired, just as crewel yarn, to create a yarn that meets size and color needs. Because the individual plies of persian yarn are more tightly twisted, it wears better than crewel yarn. It works well for both needlepoint and surface embroidery, but is most often associated with canvas work.

For many years there was a wool persian sold which had five plies loosely twisted together. This yarn is no longer generally available, but may be found in some shops.

There is a synthetic, or man-made, persian-type yarn available on a somewhat limited basis. It pills easily and generally forms stitches which are less attractive than wool. It is, however, less expensive than the wool.

◆ There are four types of cotton threads which are generally available for needlework: *stranded cotton, pearl cotton, matte cotton,* and *flower thread*. Each of these threads is produced by more than one manufacturer.

EMBROIDERY FLOSS, STRANDED COTTON, and FLOSS are all common names for the same thread. It is sold in eight-meter skeins. A full thread is composed of six smaller strands which, in turn, are each made up of two plies. The six strands are easily separated so that you can combine them and use as many as needed to achieve the coverage you desire. It comes in

hundreds of colors. Stranded cotton is one of the most versatile embroidery threads.

Recently there have been some difficulties with stranded cottons in dark reds, navy, and black. Some are proving not to be color-fast. This is not limited to one brand, but has been found to be a common problem with the thread from several companies. It is wise to check these strong colors to be certain that excess dye has been removed.

PEARL COTTON, COTON PERLE, or PERLE COTON is a tightly twisted thread with fairly high sheen. It has a wide color range. There are three thicknesses, or diameters, that are generally available. These are sized by number, #3 is the heaviest, #8 the finest, and #5 falls between the two. Some people remember that number three is thickest by associating the letter 't' with the two words.

#12 pearl cotton, which is even finer than #8, is gaining popularity as its color range has been expanded. Care should be taken not to use overly long strands of any size pearl cotton. Drawing a strand repeatedly through the ground will cause it to lose its sheen.

MATTE COTTON is rather loosely twisted. As the name states, it has a mat, or dull, finish. Color range is good, but somewhat limited. Because of the loose twist this thread tends to fray easily.

DANISH FLOWER THREAD is more tightly twisted than matte cotton, however it also has a mat finish. The thread was originally imported from Denmark for counted work on linen. There is now at least one brand manufactured and distributed by a United States company.

◆ If the working thread is composed of several, easily divisible, smaller parts, be sure to separate them. This is called *stripping* the thread. Put

these strands back together again before stitching, or use the number necessary for the particular stitch. The procedure produces a much better looking stitch. It also means that the ground will be well covered with fewer strands, which generally contributes to an improved appearance. It is one process that is well worth your time.

To strip a length of thread: With one hand, hold the piece near the top. Select one of the small strands with the other hand, and pull straight up. If the remaining strands 'bunch up,' smooth them out before removing another one. Pulling one of the small strands sideways to remove it, rather than pulling straight up, is almost sure to create a tangle. Be sure to pull straight up and smooth out the remaining strands.

Continue pulling out strands. Be sure to straighten those remaining before removing others.

◆ A help for stripping cotton threads is a small piece of regular felt. Wet the felt, and wring out all excess water. It should be just slightly damp. Place the damp felt around the end of thread to be stripped. Hold the two in your non-dominant hand. With dominant hand, pull out plies, one at a time. Each ply will be just barely damp so it will dry in a very short time. Continue to strip thread and then stitch as usual. Some stitchers feel that the slight dampness will help threads to lay straighter on the ground material.

The above method can also be used for silk threads, but be sure to first check that the dyes are fast when dampened. Test a small piece of the thread on a wet paper towel.

◆ Tightly twisted threads such as pearl cotton are very seldom separated. Certainly, a given design can require an exception to this.

◆ Drawing a strand of pearl cotton over a slightly moistened sponge or piece of damp felt will eliminate the crimps and twists that frequently

cause this thread to knot. Use a clean, washed sponge, not a new one that has just been rinsed. New sponges contain a chemical to prevent them from drying out. Washing should remove that chemical. Make sure that the sponge is just moistened. You do not want to soak the thread, just barely dampen it. Allow the thread to dry completely before stitching. The process makes working with pearl cotton much easier, and the thread also seems to lie flatter on the ground fabric.

Dampening will also remove the crimp and twist from other threads, such as silk or nylon. Sometimes you will want to stitch with the threads while they are slightly damp. Try this on a scrape of fabric before doing it on your piece.

◆   For projects which require many colors, use several needles. Thread each with a different color. When not using them, place the threaded needles in a pin cushion or piece of paper. If you note the color number on the paper, it will be easy to find the correct thread. This system means it is not necessary to stop stitching and thread a needle each time a new color is needed. Your needles and colors are ready, waiting for you.

◆   If there is a long tail of thread beyond the eye of the needle, be sure to keep moving the needle along it as you stitch. If it is not moved frequently, the thread will fray where it passes through the eye.

◆   Do not use an overly long length of thread. A long strand will mar, fray, become dirty, lose its luster, and generally create an unsatisfactory stitch. If the stitch is a long one and the thread does not tend to damage easily, you can use a longer length. Small stitches and more delicate threads require shorter strands. These suggestions will change depending on the stitch pattern and design priorities.

◆   How long a thread you use depends on the type of thread it is and the stitch being worked. A rule of thumb is a strand 18″ to 20″ long.

While you may not always have a measuring tape with you to determine the length of thread, you do have your arm. It can help if you have measured it before you need to cut a thread.

Hold a measuring tape between the thumb and forefinger of your dominate hand. Extend your arm. Measure from your thumb to the inside of your elbow, and from thumb to shoulder. Since the traditional measure of extended arm to nose may not be a yard for your reach, measure this length also. When you need to cut a thread a given length, you will have a standard against which to compare.

◆ We all rip. Someone said that if you are not ripping, you are not improving. Elsa Williams, a legend in embroidery, frequently said, "Ripping keeps you humble." As a general rule, do not reuse the thread you rip for new stitches. This used thread usually creates stitches with an unsatisfactory appearance.

◆ If you have stitched right down to the last inch of thread, and do not have enough left to anchor, try this. Use a scrap of thread five to six inches long. Thread both ends into the eye of a needle. On the back of the fabric, run the needle under the stitches where you want to anchor your working thread, but leave the loop of the scrap thread loose. Pass the short working thread into the loop. Gently pull the ends of the scrap thread through the stitches which will serve as the anchor, pulling with them the loop and end of working thread. It sounds complicated, but is actually simple. Just be gentle

The same idea works if the short piece of thread is still on top of the ground fabric and you want it on the under side. Pass the needle with the ends of the scrap thread through to the back of the fabric. Leave the loop on the surface. Place the short end of the working thread through the loop. Gently pull the scrap thread ends to the back of the ground. The loop, with the end of the working thread in it, will follow.

◆ Always assume that a thread will bleed in water. Even if you do not plan to get the design wet, it is wise to know if the threads are colorfast. Wet a piece of paper towel so that it is soaked. Fold the towel with a snip of the thread between the layers. Allow to dry. If there is even the slightest discoloration on the dry towel, the thread is not colorfast.

◆ *Dye lot* refers to the number or letter assigned to a group of threads, or yarn, all of which were dyed at the same time. Threads colored together in the same dye bath, with the same chemical strength, and for the same length of time, have the same intensity and value. Various dye lots can display a great deal of deviation.

The threads dyed, for instance on Monday, will likely be different from those dyed on Tuesday, even if they are the same color and the same yarn. This difference could conceivably present a problem. Perhaps you purchase project yarn which was dyed on Monday and run out. When you return to the store, the only thread they have of the same kind and color was dyed on Tuesday. Almost always there will be a distinct difference in the colors and/or values, which will be very apparent in the needlework.

It is very important to purchase sufficient yarn of the same dye lot for your project. Most experts suggest buying a bit extra, just in case you need more. Make a note of the dye lot or save thread labels for future reference. Then, if you do need more yarn, at least you know the dye lot you used at the beginning.

Dye lot differences are especially a problem with the natural threads made of cotton, linen, wool or silk. Man-made threads, because their construction is controlled in the manufacturing process, are less likely to have diverse dye colorings. However, do not assume that because a thread is man-made, it is therefore immune to dye lot changes.

There are some threads available which are said to be *dye lot matched*. This indicates that no matter when the thread was dyed, all lots of the same color will be of identical value. While matched dye lots are not

impossible, such statements should be viewed with skepticism. It may be true that all lots will be a perfect color match, but it would be wise to check this for yourself.

◆ It happens to almost every embroiderer, sooner or later, you realize that you are running out of your thread's dye lot. And generally, your local needlework shop will have just sold the last of that lot number. The most important thing you can do is to *stop stitching* before you use all that thread.

Purchase more thread in the dye lot closest to yours. Take a piece of the old thread with you when you shop. Lay it in among the threads of various lots. The shop will probably have several dye lots of your thread in stock, so be sure to compare all of them. Take the threads to a window, if possible. Colors look different in daylight.

Mix the old and the new dye lots together. If you are stitching with three strands in your needle, do several rows with two strands of the old and one of the new. Then several with one strand old, two new. And, finally, all new dye lot.

It is not a perfect answer — the best solution is to have just the right amount of your dye lot — but it will ease the transition from old to new.

◆ When testing a skein of thread proves it is not colorfast, there may be a way to salvage it. Soak the entire skein in lukewarm water. The thread will be less apt to become tangled if you leave it uncut. Remove any labels and hold the strands together with a twister at each end of the thread loop. Change the water frequently, until it stays totally clear and all excess dye has been removed from the thread. This can take several days. Blot, and dry away from sunlight and heat. Then try the colorfast test again to be certain no extra dye remains in the thread.

◆ Should the thread still bleed after the water bath, you can try white vinegar. Start with 50% vinegar and 50% water in a bowl large enough to hold the skein without crowding. Soak several hours or overnight. If these proportions do not stop the bleeding, try increasing the vinegar to 75%. Rinse well, blot, and allow to dry. Again try the colorfast test. If, after using the vinegar and water, the thread still bleeds, it would be wise to use a different color or, if necessary, a different thread.

◆ Just because one dye lot of a thread is colorfast, does not mean that all dye lots will be. Because one color of a thread is colorfast, does not mean that all colors will also be. And, even though a thread is colorfast in water, it may not be if it comes in contact with chemicals such as those in glue.

◆ If you get a piece of finished needlework wet, and the thread starts to bleed, do not allow the fabric to dry. Keep it submerged in water. Continue to rinse in cool water until the water is clear and bleeding stops. It may not be possible to remove all stains from the ground fabric, but this is the best system to try.

◆ No matter how careful you are, sometimes 'thread knots' develop. These are small, pesky knots which form between the eye of the needle and where the thread is connected to the ground fabric. There almost always is a loop beyond the knot.

There is no sure answer for these knots, but one way frequently works to undo them. Hold the thread in both hands, with the thread knot and loop about in the center. Pull slightly, to put just a bit of tension on the thread and loop — not too much. If you pull too hard you will just succeed in making the knot tighter. The loop should lean toward one hand or the other.

Put the point of the needle into the loop *from the direction which the loop favors*. Do not draw the needle through the loop, but just pull the loop slightly with the point. Pull toward the direction in which the needle is pointing. Often this will cause the knot to release. Thus, if

the loop leans toward the right, insert the needle from the right and give a gentle tug to the left.

PUT THE POINT OF THE NEEDLE INTO THE LOOP <u>FROM</u> THE DIRECTION THE LOOP LEANS TOWARD.

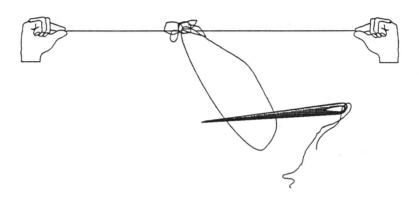

It can not be emphasized enough, put the point of the needle in the loop from the direction to which the loop leans. If you insert the needle point in the opposite direction, you will cause the knot to become even tighter.

Logic tells us that since one end of the thread is connected to your embroidery, and the other is in the needle, this knot should never happen. Or at worst, it should release easily. Sometimes neither is true. They are going to happen, so it is best not to let them get to you. If a bit of playing around does not dislodge the knot, it is generally best to end off before the knot and start with fresh thread.

IMPLEMENTS

◆ There are many different needles used for embroidery, but in short, tapestry needles have blunt points. The others have sharp points.

◆ The purpose of a needle is to separate the ground fabric so that the thread may pass through. A sharp needle is needed to open a closely woven fabric to make room for the thread's passage through it. Open weave grounds, such as canvas, generally have large enough fabric holes so that it is not necessary to enlarge a hole for the thread. A blunt needle is used in these cases. Rule of thumb is, if there are fairly large holes in the weave of the fabric, use a blunt needle. Dense fabrics, or techniques for which the needle must pierce the fabric threads, require a sharp needle.

◆ While the needle should prepare a hole for the thread, it must not be so large that it will leave a permanent perforation in the ground fabric. The fabric should, generally, close around the thread. Canvas, because it has fairly stable holes, does not require this adjustment.

◆ The eye of the needle must be large enough to accommodate the thread, so that it is not frayed by the sides of the eye. If the needle's eye is too large, the thread will slip out. Part of the joy of needlework is lost if you have to keep rethreading the needle because it is too big for the thread. Having to stop stitching and rethread a needle can be a cause of major frustration.

◆ The sizing of embroidery needles varies by the type. One constant is that the higher the number, the finer the needle. Thus, a #26 needle is finer and thinner than a #18.

◆ The first needles were probably thorns which simply made the holes through which the 'thread' was pulled. Today we have the luxury of a wide variety of needle types. Most are made by machine. A very few, used mostly for Japanese embroidery, are hand-made. The following is limited to the machine made, hand needles used for general embroidery.

TAPESTRY needles are medium length, with a long eye. They come in #13, #18, #20, #22, #24, #26, and #28. They are excellent for various counted thread techniques including canvas work. Their blunt point separates the ground threads, generally without piercing them. Be aware that the finer sizes, even though they are blunt, can draw blood.

CHENILLE needles are sharp. They come in sizes #22, #24, and #26. They are the same length and diameter as tapestry needles. They have the same size and shape eye as do tapestry needles. The #26 chenille has just recently become readily available.

CREWEL needles are sharp and, opposed to chenilles, are fairly short. They also have a more rounded eye than the chenilles. Sizing is #1, #2, #3, #4, #5, #6, #7, #8, #9, and #10.

QUILTING or QUILTING, BETWEEN needles are very short and sharp. They have a round eye and are available in sizes #5, #6, #7, #8, #9, #10, and #12. Sizes #5 — #7 tend to be larger than most quilters are comfortable with; the #8 — #9 are more often used. #10 and #12 are very fine. Generally these are used for quilting, although some embroiderers use them to attach beads to their work.

APPLIQUE needles are used in quilting. They are longer than the quilting needles described above, however, they come in the same diameter and size number as quilting needles. (Technically 'applique' is written with an accent over the e — appliqué. In common usage today, the accent is almost always dropped.)

BEADING needles are long, extremely fine, and easily bent or broken. They are used, as their name indicates, for attaching beads.

There are two types of beading needles, a basic needle which resembles other needles, and twisted wires, or straws. 'Straws' is the name for twisted wires which is found frequently in European work and texts. Twisted wires are most often used for stringing beads, but occasionally also for embroidery.

Regular beading needle sizes are #10, #12, #13, and #15. The finest is #15, and it is extremely fine. The numbers correspond to seed beads. Thus, if a #10 seed bead is being used, a #10 needle would be correct. If a #11 seed bead is right for the needlework, either a #10 or #12 needle would be appropriate, since there is no #11 needle.

◆ Other needles are available, including long and short darners, millinery, and leather needles. They are specialized, and thus are explored in the classes or texts where they are recommended.

◆ Keep needles away from moisture. If they were placed in a black paper when you bought them, that paper may be impregnated with an agent to keep them dry. Store them in the same paper.

◆ If you have lost the paper the needles came in, or if you just want to have all your needles together, keep them in a container of some sort. You might want one of the lovely, ornate needle cases which can be found at needlework shops. There are small plastic boxes that have a magnetic base. Or you possibly will want a beautiful wood box with a magnetic insert. Using the magnet does not hurt the needles, and helps to keep them in the box, rather than buried in your chair. All of these are available at needlework shops.

- An alternate container for your needles is a small bottle, such as the type in which prescriptions are dispensed. If storing sharp needles in such a container, put cotton or a piece of felt in the bottom. It will protect the points.

- Some like to store their needles in a piece of felt, or the felt pages of a needle book. This felt may, or may not, be treated with an agent to help keep them dry. If you only put the same size and type needle on each piece of felt, it is easy to keep them separated.

- According to some stitchers, natural wool felt is the only acceptable material in which to store needles. The reasoning is that chemicals in man-made felt will cause the needles to rust.

- No matter how you store your needles, it will be a help if you keep them sorted by type and size. A bit of care will save time when you are looking for the right needle for a project.

- It is very important to keep needles dry and away from all forms of moisture. They will rust quickly if not kept dry. Special care should be taken in areas that have high humidity.

- *Desiccants* contain a drying agent powder which fights moisture and thus, the damage from it. The powder is in a small package, about an inch square. They are used in many products, including the large, stock bottles of pills and tablets from which prescriptions are filled in a pharmacy. If asked, a pharmacist will sometimes give you one of these packets at no charge. Put a desiccant in with stored needles to keep them dry and protected from rust.

- There are three ways to thread a needle: folding the thread, using a tiny paper, and a commercial threader. They will all work. Each

embroiderer must decide for themselves which is appropriate for the thread being used.

FOLD METHOD TO THREAD NEEDLE: Near the end of the thread which will go into the eye, fold the thread over the eye end of the needle. Hold the needle so that the thread is creased over the edge, not the opening, of the eye. With the thumb and forefinger of dominate hand, slide thread off the edge of the needle's eye. Pinch so that the thread fold is hidden between your thumb and finger. With non-dominate hand, place needle against the flesh holding thread, with the eye opening generally above where thread is. Gently push eye of needle down between thumb and finger, and over thread fold. This is easier than it sounds, but does take some practice. Since you can not see the thread between your thumb and forefinger, it is rather like threading the needle on faith. With practice this system will work, and work very well.

PAPER METHOD TO THREAD NEEDLE: Cut a tiny strip of paper, just slightly narrower than the length of the needle's eye, and about two inches long. Fold the strip, end to end, with the tail of the thread in the crease of the fold. Push the folded paper through the eye of the needle, and with it, the thread.

COMMERCIAL NEEDLE THREADERS: There are three basic types of manufactured threaders. One has a wire to place through the needle's eye. Put the thread through the loop of wire, and pull it, along with the thread, back through the eye.

The second type is a flat piece of metal with two holes in it. The end with one hole is placed through the eye, the thread put through the hole, and the threader pulled back through the eye. The thread is left in the eye of the needle. One end of this threader has a larger hole for bigger needles, the other is smaller to help thread finer needles.

The third type of commercial threader has a small hook on one end. The hook is placed through the eye, the thread caught in the hook, and threader and thread are drawn through the eye.

◆ Many embroiderers find a heavy commercial threader to be indispensable for threading metallic threads.

◆ There is another way to thread tightly twisted threads such as pearl cotton. Lay the thread over the fleshy part of the index finger of your non-dominate hand. Place the eye of the needle over the thread. Pressing the eye against your finger and the thread, push the needle upward. A thread loop should form at the opening of the eye. Grasp this loop and pull thread completely through the eye.

Some embroiderers find it easier to 'scrub' the needle gently backward and forward over the thread and finger. A small thread loop will come through the eye. The thread can then be pulled completely through the eye.

◆ However you thread your needle, if you are having trouble, try turning the needle around and threading from the other side. When the die which creates the eye opening is forced through the needle, one side is a bit smoother and larger than the other. It is generally easier to thread from the smooth, slightly larger side. Also on the same smooth side, the groove directly below the eye is just a bit longer and deeper. It will help to guide the thread into the eye.

◆ Only stitch with a clean, shiny needle. Dull or oxidized needles can leave dark spots on your embroidery. Some people have a chemical in their systems which causes needles to darken. If this is a problem for you, try periodically passing the needle through an emery. Emery is a powder which will clean needles. It is generally sold as a pin cushion or in a small strawberry shape.

◆   Some stitchers like to use a dryer softener sheet to keep their needles clean. Just wipe each needle with the softener sheet. Keep a small piece of the dryer sheet with your needlework supplies. You can clean all needles used whenever you finish a stitching session.

◆   Some embroiderers like to run the needle they are stitching with through their hair at least once every stitching session. They say that natural oils in the hair keep the needle from oxidation. Care should be taken to avoid scalp injury.

◆   The cost of a new needle is fairly small. If you use an oxidized needle you run the risk of leaving a permanent black spot on your embroidery. To avoid using a new needle, when necessary, could be false economy.

◆   A *needle gripper*, or *needle puller*, can make pulling a needle through a tight place much easier. It is simply a piece of rubber which is placed around the needle. This makes the needle easier to hold, and gives your fingers greater pulling power. You can purchase a rubber circle for just this purpose at many needlework shops. You can also use a piece of a balloon, a rubber band, or cut a circle from an old rubber glove.

◆   Never 'park' a needle in the ground material within the design area of your needlework. It might leave puncture marks that cannot be removed and will spoil the finished project. Or if you do not get back to the piece as soon as you expect, a permanent rust spot could form on the ground fabric.

◆   When buying needles for a new project, get several extra. It is a fact of an embroiderer's life that needles disappear.

◆ If your ground fabric is on a working frame, attach the end of a small piece of felt to the edge. Thumb tack it in place through the ground material, into the edge of the frame, either at the top or bottom. Be sure to keep it completely out of the design area. This is the place to park the extra needles you need for that particular project, but are not currently using.

◆ Try to keep a bit of thread in each needle you are working with, even if you have parked it to one side. Then, if the needle slips and falls, it is much easier to find. The bit of colored thread can more easily be seen than just a needle.

◆ Instead of a piece of fabric attached to the project into which you park needles, try working a fat Rhodes stitch or a thick, oblong cross stitch, outside the design area at the edge of the ground fabric. Needles that need to be placed temporarily aside can be put into either of these padded stitches.

◆ A *trolley needle* is not truly a stitching needle at all. It is a style of laying tool, used to help straighten the plies or strands of thread as they are stitched. It resembles a large, blunt, #13 tapestry needle attached to a type of collar which fits around a finger. The needle section extends about an inch beyond the end of your finger.

Trolley needles have the potential of being dangerous. It is easy to forget one is being worn. Eye damage can result when moving, or relaxing, the hand.

◆ Thimbles are considered a necessary evil by some, loved by others. They are used to protect a finger from the constant pressure of pushing a needle through ground fabric. At one time, they were standard equipment for quilters.

A thimble may be strictly utilitarian or beautifully ornate. Modern ones are made of plastic, leather, or metal; antiques are generally of ivory, glass, horn or mother of pearl. Some thimbles have an open area at the end to accommodate a longer fingernail.

◆   When doing any needlework which causes pressure from the needle, or the thread, at the same place on your finger, try a rubber finger. These are designed to make it easier to flip through a stack of papers and are available in office supply stores. They are a wonderful way to protect the sore place on your finger.

◆   Use a label to make life easier when doing bead work. A self-stick label, pulled just part way from the backing paper, presents a slightly sticky side. Pick up several beads by placing the tacky surface into the package of beads. They will stay on the back of the label until you release one with the tip of your needle. This is a much neater system than having beads skirting all over your work area.

◆   Carry the above sticky label idea one step further. Completely remove the label from the backing paper. With double-faced tape, attach the label to the unopened end of a can, sticky side up. Any can with a rim will work. The rim will help keep the beads in place and, by putting the can on end, raise the beads to a more comfortable working level.

◆   You need three pairs of cutting instruments for needlework. A pair of long shears is perfect for cutting fabric or canvas. Have two pairs of embroidery scissors. The best pair should be used for cutting soft threads such as cotton, linen, wool, or silk. If you save this pair just for soft threads, they will stay sharp longer.

Keep a second pair of embroidery scissors for cutting metal, metallics, and man-made threads. Such threads will rapidly dull scissors. If you get a new pair of embroidery scissors, do not discard the old ones. Delegate them to those threads which are harder to cut.

◆   When you are in class, or away from home working on needlework, and you have only one pair of scissors with you, there is a way to save them and cut all the threads necessary. Cut the cotton, linen, wool, and silk threads with the tips of those scissors. Cut metals, metallics, and other man-made threads back near the screw adjustment where the blades are connected. That way you will keep the points sharp.

◆   Our hands are vital to our needlework, but they can also be the vehicle by which dirt is carried. <u>Wash</u> them before you begin to stitch. Dirt can very easily be transferred from hands to threads or fabrics. Never read the newspaper, and then begin your work, without washing your hands first. Your fingers pick up newsprint which transfers to ground fabric and threads. The same is true of the ink used for magazines. It takes just a minute to wash your hands before you begin stitching. It is well worth your time.

◆   Conservationists tell us that to be certain our embroidery will last for generations, it is best not to use hand lotions or creams just before stitching. The chemicals in them can cause future damage to the threads and ground fabric.

◆   Rough hands can be a problem when stitching with some threads. Smooth the rough spots by using one of the products design to remove callouses from feet and hands. You can find them in a drug store or pharmacy.

Miracle Whip Salad Dressing also works well to remove rough spots that cause problems when stitching. Rub about one teaspoon into your hands. Wait five minutes. Then rub hands together, briskly, over a sink. The rough skin will come off easily. Some like to add a teaspoon of sugar or salt to the Miracle Whip. Be *sure* to wash hands thoroughly with soap and warm water before stitching.

◆   A hoop with a screw adjustment is generally preferred over one which has a spring adjustment. The screw will permit more precise tension on the outer ring of the hoop. Old fashioned spring adjustment-type hoops are frequently metal. The metal easily rusts and will leave marks on fabric. Instead of the metal spring type, consider a wood hoop with screw adjustment.

◆   There is a hoop which has a plastic outer ring, with a metal rod for the inner ring. The inner metal ring acts as a type of spring to hold the fabric in place.

      Such metal/plastic hoops are hard on ground fabric. They have only one tension which is very tight. This places a great deal of stress on the material. Consider, carefully, if the ground fabric can withstand the stress before using these hoops.

◆   Another type of hoop has both the inner and outer rings made of plastic. The inner ring has an extended lip which overlaps the top edge of the outer ring. These usually have a screw adjustment. Such plastic hoops are generally acceptable. Some embroiderers feel these hoops are too heavy to hold during long stitching sessions, others find them just perfect.

◆   Wooden hoops may be a bit more expensive, but are very adaptable to various weights of ground fabrics. They are light weight, easy to handle, and because of their screw adjustment, it is easy to regulate the tension.

◆   When using a hoop, first wrap both rings in gauze strips. Such wrapping will keep the chemicals in the wood away from your ground. It will also cushion the hoop and prevent breaking the fibers of the ground. Gauze, about one inch wide, works well. Start at the screw adjustment and wrap round and round the hoop ring. It is not necessary to have many layers of gauze. Just slightly over-lap it as you wrap.

When you reach the screw adjustment where you started, a couple of stitches will hold all in place. Do the same with the inner ring. Gauze strips can be found at most drug stores in the first aid department.

◆ For an alternate method to keep the hoop from contact with your ground, cut two circles of fabric. They may be washed muslin, cotton, or even cotton blend. The pieces should be about two to four inches larger than the diameter of the hoop. An eight-inch hoop requires two circles ten to twelve inches in diameter.

In the center of each circle, cut a hole two inches smaller than the hoop. These holes would be six inches across in the example above. You have created two fabric shapes which resemble donuts.

Sandwich your embroidery between the two circles of fabric, and place in the hoop. The wood of the hoop will be in contact with the fabric donuts, and not touch the ground fabric.

◆ When stitching on delicate fabrics such as satins or silks, place acid free tissue paper between the ground and the hoop. Tear away the paper in the center of the hoop, exposing the area for embroidery.

◆ Yet another way to cushion ground material from the pressure of a hoop is place a paper towel on the fabric in the area to be stitched. Position the hoop over the toweling. After the hoop is in place, tear away the towel in the section to be stitched. The paper toweling remaining between the ground material and hoop ring will act as a cushion to help prevent hoop marks.

◆ Wash your hoops occasionally to remove skin oils and residue. These can mar your fabric.

◆ If you plan to hold the hoop in your hand, as opposed to using a frame holder or frame weight to support it, select one with as small a diameter as feasible. The smaller size will mean less weight and assures that the fingers of the holding hand can reach the center of the work to assist the stitching hand. Take into consideration the size of the stitches and, if applicable, the count of the fabric, when deciding which hoop to use. In general, smaller hoops will suit more delicate fabrics, and heavier materials will be better held in a slightly larger hoop.

◆ Right-handed embroiderers who hold a hoop in their left hand, will usually be most comfortable holding a hoop with the screw adjustment at the 10:00 o'clock position. Left-handed people, holding the hoop in their right hand, will want to place the screw at the 2:00 o'clock location.

◆ Never, never leave your work in a hoop when you are not working on it, even if you have wrapped the rings in gauze. Leaving the fabric stretched in a hoop, even over a short period of time, can cause the fibers of the material to break. It is almost certain that you will end up with permanent hoop marks.

◆ If you wish to work on a piece of canvas or fabric which needs to be mounted on a working frame, but is too small to fit usual frame sizes, a hoop can be used.

Select a hoop three to four inches larger than the ground fabric. Place a piece of waste material, such as muslin, in the hoop. Baste the ground fabric on top of the center of the material in the hoop. Carefully cut the waste material away from behind the piece of ground fabric. This process creates a window in the waste material. The window is covered with the ground fabric that is to be stitched. Proceed with stitching as usual.

◆ There are several markers that may be used to transfer a design to your ground fabric.

Permanent markers especially designed for needlework can be found where embroidery supplies are sold. One brand is Nepo. They have a medium-fine point and come in several colors. Some people feel that a line made with one of these pens bleeds out into the fabric. This can cause wide outlines which must be covered with stitching.

♦ Regular permanent inks are frequently acceptable. Stationery and office supply stores carry Pilot SC-UF pens. They form a very fine line. For many years these have been used to mark designs on ground fabric. The disadvantage is that, currently, they are only available in black. A dark line may be difficult to cover with stitches.

♦ Micron Pigma pens, by Sakura, are usually sold in art supply stores. They come in various widths and several colors. The company says they are permanent, smudge-proof, waterproof, and fade resistant. These pens have recently gained great favor for marking ground fabric.

♦ India ink has long been used to draw the design on ground fabric. Many embroidery instructors still use this method. It does have a tendency to be messy, but with practice can prove very acceptable. India ink creates a very black line which will possibly be difficult to cover with stitches.

♦ Some instructors and needleartists like to use an exceptionally hard graphite pencil. These are usually found in art supply stores. They are identified by '4H,' or the even harder one, '5H.' The marks they make can be difficult to remove, and the graphite can cling to light colored threads, yarns, and the ground, itself. A hard pencil might, however, be the perfect marker for you.

There are many brands of pencils sold in art supply stores. Some of these pencils are extremely hard and excellent for marking most ground materials.

◆ Both air soluble and water soluble pens are usually available in fabric and needlework stores. They are each rather controversial in the embroidery world.

◆ The air soluble pen has a medium lavender ink. It is formulated to react to humidity in the air. Marks made with this pen will generally fade in 24 to 48 hours. This characteristic limits the time available to stitch a drawn design, or a given section of the design. Heavy applications of the pen may become permanent.

◆ Water soluble pens generally have a light blue ink, although there is at least one with pink colored ink. The marks made with them are visible until dampened with water. They may have to be dampened, and allowed to dry, several times before the marks are completely removed. Dense, dark lines are more difficult to remove. Sometimes these heavy lines will become permanent. In high humidity the lines will fade, although this is a slow process.

◆ Both the air and water soluble pens have been manufactured for about ten years. They were originally designed to be used on non-porous ground fabrics, such as synthetics. This ink would not be absorbed by the fibers of the fabric. Ground fabrics made of natural fibers are more absorbent.

◆ It is important that all chemicals of air and water soluble pens be completely removed. If this is not done, there is the potential of problems years after the stitching is finished. Incompletely removed lines have been known to 'come back' in the form of brown marks. Heat, either from an iron or even direct sunlight, must be avoided, or the marks will become permanent.

◆ Manufacturers of air and water soluble pens say they have reformulated their inks so that they are easier to remove. They are thus less

likely to cause long-term damage. Many needleartists are currently reporting excellent results, providing the air and water soluble inks are completely removed. All traces of the ink coloring agent must be eliminated, either by washing the ground fabric or by dampening it.

◆ There are also temporary marking systems. These include pouncing, which involves creating dotted lines of powder by sifting it through perforations in a paper pattern, as well as the use of various colored chalks.

◆ The decision of which marking instrument to use is extremely important. The type of fabric to be marked should be considered. The same method that would be proper for use on the linen twill ground for crewel work, possibly will not be appropriate for the canvas ground of needlepoint.

◆ Ball point pens are <u>never</u> satisfactory as needlework markers.

◆ Do not use any type of marking instrument on your fabric until you have tested it on a scrap of the same material. Even if the word 'permanent' is on the label, it does not necessarily mean the mark will be permanent on your ground material with your threads.

Draw a line on the scrap fabric, allow to dry, then try to rub it off. Rub with a white paper towel or white cloth. Then wet the line and rub again. If even the tiniest bit of mark comes off on the paper, do not use that marker for your embroidery.

◆ Whichever marking method you use, be sure to apply it with a light hand. Do not press hard. Keep the lines as fine as possible, while still being able to see them. Remember that if using a permanent marker, the lines will have to be hidden with stitching. It is frequently difficult

to cover heavy, dark lines, especially with light value threads. Always follow the directions, if any, which come with a marker.

◆ When transferring a design to the ground fabric, it helps to have light coming from behind it. Tape the paper design to a window, then center the ground fabric and tape it on top of the paper design. The light coming through the window is frequently enough that the design lines can be seen through the ground. It is then easy to trace them on the fabric.

◆ A light table is especially useful when drawing an outline on ground fabric. A light table is simply a box with light positioned so that it comes from behind the top surface. The master design is placed on the table, the ground fabric on top of it. Because the light is behind, it is easier to see the lines on the master and trace them on the ground. Commercial light tables are available, but generally are quite expensive.

◆ An inexpensive light table is simply a clean piece of glass or plastic suspended between two tables of equal height. A lamp without the shade is placed below the glass or plastic. With the back light source thus created, proceed to position the design and ground fabric as described above.

◆ An alternative to two tables is to open the two sides of a table which has leaves. Remove the leaves. Place the glass or plastic across the opening. Or, try a glass topped table. This last option eliminates the need for an additional piece of glass or plastic.

◆ If you are going to work your needlework on a frame, you have two basic choices. They are called working frames because they hold the needlework while it is being stitched.

There is a roller-type (scroll) frame which has dowels at the top and bottom, and rigid side bars. The dowels have tapes attached. The ground fabric is sewn to the tapes on the top and bottom dowels. The rigid side bars keep the fabric stretched tightly from top to bottom. Sometimes it helps to lace the sides of the fabric to the side bars. Such lacing will put a horizontal tension on the fabric. When it is pulled from all four sides, the fabric on a scroll frame is quite tight.

A scroll frame is especially useful if the design is large. As the work progresses, the ground fabric can be rolled on to either of the dowels so that a different section is exposed for stitching.

◆   Do not use a scroll frame if stitches will be disturbed by rolling over the top or bottom dowels. Delicate silks or metals could be permanently damaged by the crushing caused when they are rolled on the dowels.

◆   Stretcher strips can be used to make working frames. Four bars are put together to form a square or rectangle, with an open area in the center. The ground fabric is attached to the bars, leaving the open center free for embroidery.

Stretcher strips are sold in sets of two of the same length. They come in two styles. One type is almost two inches wide. These are artist's bars, used for the type of canvas that is the base for oil painting. If you buy these strips to make a 10″ x 12″ frame, the outside edge of the frame will be 10″ x 12″, the inside opening will be considerably smaller.

The other type of strip is about one-half inch wide, and called needlework bars. If you buy a set ten inches long, and one set twelve inches long, the inside area will be just slightly smaller than 10″ x 12″. Needlework bars should be used for embroidery, not artist's stretcher strips. Purchase them where you buy needlework supplies.

◆   To attach ground fabric to a stretcher type working frame, use thumb tacks rather than staples. If a frame is being used, then it follows that the ground material needs to be stretched very tightly at all times. Just the act of stitching on it will cause it to 'give' and become slack. You will have to re-stretch the ground at least once during the working time. It is much easier to remove and reinsert thumb tacks than to remove staples. In addition, staples do not hold the fabric as firmly as do the thumb tacks.

Begin to attach ground material to the stretcher bars by putting a tack in the middle of each of the four sides. Pull the fabric as tightly as possible. Put a tack on either side of the four center tacks. Continuing to pull tightly, work to the end of each side of the frame by putting tacks on either side of those in the center. This helps to keep a tight, even tension on the ground fabric.

Thumb tacks should be no more than one-half inch apart. If further apart, they will not hold the ground fabric securely. When stitching causes the ground to become slack, and it will, it is seldom necessary to remove and re-do more than two adjacent sides to return it to the original tension.

◆   During the process of stitching, the ground material will become slack. It is important to re-tighten it. This is easy if the work is on stretcher strips. Remove the thumb tacks from two adjacent sides. Replace the tacks, pulling the fabric tightly as you do so. On a scroll frame, loose fabric can be tightened by redoing the side lacing or turning the end dowel bars.

◆   If the ground material becomes slack and, for whatever reason, you are unable to tighten it on the frame as described above, try unsharpened pencils. Force a pencil between the ground fabric and the top of the stretcher bars. Two pencils, one on each of two adjacent sides, will probably be enough to increase the tension of the fabric. This is a temporary, stopgap, measure. As soon as possible remove and replace tacks to properly tighten the ground fabric.

◆ A frame holder is one of several different items that helps to hold the working frame. This permits both hands to be free to work the embroidery.

◆ A frame can be attached to the holder which sits on top of your lap. Or, the holder can slip under your thigh. Both support the working frame about six to twelve inches above your lap. Generally, the holder will adjust the frame so that it is perpendicular to your body, or tilted at whatever angle is best for you. Purchase these frame holders in needlework shops.

◆ A floor stand also holds a working frame. As its name states, this frame holder sits on the floor. They usually can be pulled close to your chair and will tilt the work to various angles. You can find them in needlework shops.

◆ Both floor stands and lap frame holders often come with their own working frames attached. Usually there is a way to alter the holder so that a stretcher bar frame, or hoop, may be attached. Sometimes adapters are available which permit you to use your own frames. Both floor and lap frame holders are available in needlework shops. They have a wide price range.

◆ Frame weights are small, heavy objects which, because of their weight, hold the working frame so that it extends beyond the edge of a table. The weights range from 3″ x 3″, to as large as the stitcher wishes them to be. The total weight is usually three to five pounds. 'Shot' such as used with guns for hunting is said to make good a good weighted filler. Pennies and sand are also excellent weights.

A frame weight can be very elaborate, covered with embellishments and found objects. Or, it can be as simple as a weighted cotton glove.

They can sometimes be purchased in needlework shops, but many stitchers make their own using a favorite needlework technique.

One side of the embroidery working frame should be placed on a table. The weight is put on top of the frame, along the outer edge. The edge of the frame is held on the table by the weight. Most of the frame extends beyond the table, giving easy access to the embroidery. It is not necessary to hold the frame in your hands. Both hands are free to stitch the needlework.

◆ Frame weights have the advantage of being small in size and, although heavy, easily portable. They go with you to class where there is almost always a table to support it. They are also a way the stitcher can display creativity. The frame weight often expresses the personality of its owner.

◆ An alternate, and very simple, frame weight, is a heavy book. Place the book on the edge of the frame, just as you would a specially created frame weight.

◆ Still another method of supporting a frame is to use a clamp purchased in hardware stores. A C-clamp, which is shaped like the letter 'C,' is one type that is easy to get, and not overly expensive. Hardware stores have other styles of clamps that will also work to hold a frame.

Most hardware clamps can grip the working frame to a table. The frame is held so that the embroidery can be reached from the top and bottom. Again, the purpose is to free both hands.

◆ A *laying tool* is anything which will help you place the threads smoothly on the ground fabric. Many stitches are worked with multiple strands in the needle. Stitches will have a better appearance if these strands are side-by-side on the fabric, rather than being twisted on top of each other. A laying tool slips under the thread as it is being drawn

to the back of the ground fabric. It helps to separate the plies/strands so that they lay flat. The method takes a bit of practice, but is well worth the effort.

◆ A laying tool can be as simple as your finger, but most embroiderers feel strongly that this is the least effective instrument. Others are: a large needle such as a #13 tapestry needle, a bodkin, a three or four inch plastic collar stay, a tekobari, or any device specifically made to serve as a laying tool.

A bodkin is a flat needle designed to thread elastic or ribbon through a casing. A tekobari is a Japanese embroidery tool, 4″ long. It is about ⅛″ in diameter, square at one end and tapering to a very fine point at the other end. Collar stays can be purchased in a fabric store, the other items in a needlework shop.

◆ *Pink hair tape* is a tape made by 3M Company. It is designed to hold damp hair in place as it dries. Because it has very little adhesive, it is frequently used to temporarily hold threads either out of the way, or in position. The lack of adhesive means that it will not leave a residue on your work. Pink hair tape can generally be found in drug stores or where hair products are sold.

◆ An alternative to pink hair tape is surgical tape. It can be found in a pharmacy or where first aid supplies are sold. Surgical tape, also, has very little adhesive. These tapes are especially helpful if you are taking a class. Since there is seldom enough time to finish a given section, the threads are held out of the way until the stitching can be completed.

Conservationists warn about these tapes. Although they leave little if any residue, they do have chemicals in them. A problem could arise over time from exposing ground fabric and threads to those chemicals.

◆ Try to test a magnifier before purchasing it. Perhaps the shop selling them will permit this, or a friend will lend you one. Magnifiers are tricky. They do not always perform for every person as stated on the box or in the advertising.

◆ There are several types of magnifiers that can help alleviate eye strain, and thus make embroidery much more enjoyable. One type, used by both embroiderers and non-stitchers, is a pair of basic magnifying glasses. These may be prescribed by your ophthalmologist and be specially ground for your prescription. Or, they may be those purchased from a drug or discount store. 'Clip-ons' attach to the top center edge of regular glasses. They are similar to clip on style sunglasses, but instead of dark lenses have clear magnifiers.

◆ Check your needlework shop for the various types of magnifiers designed for close work and embroidery. They usually have a round lens, four to six inches in diameter. Such magnifiers include those which clip on the edge of a working frame, sit or clamp on an adjacent table, or sit on the floor. Some have a separate light anchored to their base. Others have a fluorescent, or halogen, bulb which encircles the magnifying lens, allowing one item to provide both magnification and light.

◆ Some stitchers like a magnifier which hangs around their neck. These are generally light-weight and comfortable.

◆ Magnifiers should be approached with caution. While they provide a wonderful aid to ease eye strain and help increase stitching technique, each type is very different. Some people experience a 'sea-sick' sensation when using one for a long period.

Each magnifier does not work the same way for all embroiderers. The decision of which type to purchase can take some investigation. Since these can also be expensive, it is time well spent. If possible, it is a

good idea to try one before making your purchase. The opinion of other stitchers can also help.

◆ Although stitching in natural daylight is sometimes sufficient, additional lighting may make your embroidery more pleasurable. For some it is vital to eye comfort. If working at night, an artificial light is a basic necessity. Light source can be as simple as a decorative table lamp or one of those specially designed for needlework.

Special lamps for close work come in many sizes, styles, and price ranges. Some are floor models, some sit on or attach to, a table, some can be anchored to a working frame. Some lamps also have a magnifying lens attached. As with a magnifier, try to test a lamp before you purchase it.

◆ Avoid working in a dark room, under the spotlight of an embroidery lamp. Keep the general room light at least equal to normal lighting. Strong contrast between the illumination on your work and the surrounding area can aggravate the eye strain you are trying to avoid.

◆ When traveling to classes away from home, pack a 100 or 150 watt bulb. Pad it well to prevent breakage. Such a bulb will be invaluable for stitching in a hotel room, because hotels usually provide only 60 watt bulbs.

Also take an extension cord. You may need it in the classroom, or the hotel room, for your embroidery lamp.

◆ Beeswax is used to strengthen threads. It is sold as a small piece, and can be found in most needlework or quilting shops. Hold the wax in one hand. Place the thread between the wax and your thumb. Pull the thread with the free hand, causing it to travel under the thumb and over the wax. Depending on the amount of thread strength needed, it may be necessary to wax more than once.

Silks are often waxed when used for couching, or holding in place, metal threads. Beadwork frequently requires the strengthening that beeswax gives threads.

Conservationists tell us that the tiny amount of beeswax transferred to threads poses no threat to the longevity of the embroidery.

◆ Frequently a teacher will tell students to bring 'usual supplies,' 'general stitching items,' or a 'just-in-case kit,' to class. These names are a few of those which cover the basic implements necessary for doing needlework. The selection of items tends to reflect the favorite technique of their owner. They may change as the owner's skill and interests alter. In general, these supplies should accompany the embroiderer to every away-from-home stitching session or class. Many stitchers keep duplicates of the more important items so that the traveling set is always ready to go. The other set stays at home.

◆ The containers for the 'usual supplies' are anything which will keep them together. These run a wide gambit from basic cardboard boxes and plastic zip bags, to refrigerator storage containers, metal boxes with exquisite surface designs, and beautiful baskets which are lined and outfitted with pockets. Frequently the container reflects the personality of its owner. Size of the holder varies depending on the volume of items being toted.

◆ A starter list of *usual stitching items* follows. Each person should evaluate these, and add or subtract with experience. In addition to these, some classes will possibly require specific equipment.

> — Scissors to be used only for natural threads.

> — Scissors for metal and metallic threads. These might also be used for paper, if absolutely necessary.

— An assortment of various sized tapestry,
  crewel, chenille, and quilting needles.

— Yarn threader to help get unruly threads into
  the needle.

— Laying tool of choice to help keep threads
  straight on the ground fabric. This might be a three
  or four inch collar stay, bodkin, tekobari, or other
  item specially made for such use.

— Sewing thread to be used for basting, both
  light and dark colors.

— Straight pins. The long, fine, glass-headed
  pins are a good, general purpose type.

— Pencils. A very hard one, #4 or #5, for
  transferring designs to fabric, and one for taking
  notes. A pen can be used for taking notes only, but
  be very careful of ink transferring to other items.

— Highlighting-type pens. These are excellent for
  accenting a section of class instructions. Be careful
  that ink from these pens is not transferred to your
  needlework.

— Tape measure and/or small, 6″ ruler. Many
  embroiderers find they want to have both available.

— Beeswax for strengthening threads.

— 3M Pink Hair Tape, or other low residue tape
  to hold threads in position, or out of stitching area.

— Fine crochet hook for removing threads.

— Tweezers. There are many regular types of

tweezers available. There are also some that fold, or are designed especially for use with embroidery. Find these specialized tweezers in needlework shops.

— Small bottle of one of the liquids which stop ground threads from fraying. There are several brands available.

— Thumb tacks for attaching ground fabric to stretcher bar-type working frames.

— Small sponge. It can be wet and then used to dampen threads so that the 'kink' is removed.

TECHNIQUES

◆ The word "embroidery" is a collective term which covers the emblishment of fabric with a needle. It includes all techniques of needlework. Embroidery is not surface stitches worked with stranded cotton floss as was done in the past on design stamped pillow cases. This latter definition is archaic and incorrect. The correct name for this work is surface stitching or surface emblishment. Canvas, crewel, quilting, and all needlework forms which create decorative designs with a threaded needle fall under the universal title of "embroidery."

◆ The title "drawn thread" indicates that ground material threads have been cut and withdrawn.

◆ "Drawn fabric" means that the ground fabric threads have been distorted, pulled out of position, to form holes. Placement of these holes forms the decorative design. Drawn fabric work is frequently referred to as 'pulled work' or 'pulled canvas' if worked on a canvas ground.

◆ When doing a French knot that, for whatever reason, does not seem to be going the way it should, stop. Do not pull the working thread tight. Once a French knot is tightened, it is almost impossible to untie. Better to stop in the middle, when it is easy to undo. You can then start again.

◆ In needlework, the definition of *applique* is to apply one piece of fabric decoration to another fabric or to another surface. In general usage, the word is correctly spelled with an accent over the e — appliqué. The accent mark is almost always dropped when the word is used in connection with embroidery.

◆   When doing an applique, other than in quilting, of just about any material such as kid, canvas, or Ultrasuede, and if the shape has a point, do not place a stitch right at the tip. It will usually shred the applique fabric, or in the case of kid, destroy the backing. Instead place stitches about $1/_{16}$" on either side of the point. When placed just slightly back from the point, the stitches will hold the applique securely and yet keep it intact.

◆   To *couch* is to anchor a heavier thread in place on the surface of the ground using stitches. Depending on the technique and the effect desired, the anchoring stitches can be straight stitches placed perpendicular to the thread being couched, or a decorative stitch can be used. Herringbone, chain, and cross stitch are just three examples of decorative couching stitches.

◆   When couching, the thread being couched is the *tramé* thread. The thread being used for the anchoring stitches is the couching thread. The anchoring stitches are the couching stitches.

◆   If you are couching a thread around an area, try to do so in a clockwise direction. Working in a clockwise direction usually produces better work for both right and left handed stitchers.

◆   Especially for blackwork or a filling stitch, begin with double the usual length working thread. Start stitching in the center of the area. Use one-half the thread as you work to one boundary. Thread up the other half, which is waiting at the center of the section, and work to the other side. Continue working each half of the thread until it is necessary to end and begin a new thread. This is a good way to center a pattern in the middle of an area without having to be concerned about anchoring beginning tails.

◆   In canvas work, and frequently with other forms of needlework, do the first row of a pattern stitch across the widest area in the direction the stitch is being worked. For instance, if doing a stitch that is worked horizontally, do that first row across the widest horizontal section of the area being stitched. Continue to finish the area below the first row, then invert work and stitch remaining area. This method helps to center a stitch pattern.

◆   Starting and ending threads is not difficult. Just use 'waste knots' 'running anchors,' and 'ending tails.'

> WASTE KNOTS or IN PATH WASTE KNOTS   One way to begin a new thread is with a waste knot. Insert thread in needle. Make a knot in the end. About an inch from where you wish to start stitching, in the direction in which you will be working, go from the front of the ground fabric to the back. Bring the needle up at the point you want to begin stitching. This will leave a knot on the FRONT of the ground. On the back will be a 'tail' between the knot and the point where you are going to work. As you stitch, the back of those first few stitches will cover the 'tail.' When you reach the knot, check the back to be sure you have covered the tail. If it has been securely anchored, clip off the knot on the front of the work. This then, is why it is called a waste knot — because it is wasted, or removed. Some call this an 'in path waste knot' since it is placed directly in line of the stitching.

> AWAY WASTE KNOTS   Occasionally it will be necessary to use an 'away waste knot.' For instance, if there is not enough room left on the line you are stitching to properly anchor a waste knot. Use the same technique you did with the waste knot, except put the knot out of the line of stitching. The knot should be four to five inches away, or well out of the design area. When stitching is completed, clip knot, thread the long tail in a needle and run it under the back of the first several stitches. This is not the preferred method to begin a thread. Running the thread

through the back of stitches already worked changes the tension of those stitches on the front of the ground fabric.

Put the knot of an away waste knot either completely outside the design, beyond any area that will show after framing, or in an area that will later be covered with stitching. If you place such knots in sections of ground fabric that will be left exposed, they may leave permanent marks or holes that will detract from the design.

ENDING TAILS When about three inches of thread remain in the needle, bring the needle from the back to the front of the ground fabric, approximately two inches ahead of the last stitch. This will leave a 'tail' between the last stitch and where the thread comes to the surface. The underside of the first few stitches worked with the new thread will cover and anchor this tail. When you reach the place where the old thread comes to the surface, clip off any excess. If a new thread is started with a waste knot, you will be working over the tail of the old thread and the tail of the new thread *at the same time*. This will cause no problem because the tension of the new stitches will allow for these tails.

RUNNING ANCHOR Begin as for a waste knot, making sure that the knot on the surface is in line with the row of stitches and about 1″ away from its start. Make several small running stitches along the line to be stitched, back toward where you wish to begin stitching. Bring thread up at starting point. Stitch as usual. Work over the running stitches, piercing some of them, if possible. Clip knot when you reach it.

This is an especially good anchor for single lines worked in stem, outline, or chain stitches.

◆ If there is not enough room in the line of stitching to place an ending tail, it is necessary to run the thread under the back of preceding stitches. When in this position, try putting the thread to be ended off in

a needle which is one or two sizes smaller than the one used for the stitching. The smaller needle will be less apt to disturb the tension on the front of stitches under which the thread is ended.

◆ WHENEVER POSSIBLE, USE WASTE KNOTS, RUNNING AN-CHORS, AND ENDING TAILS. The method of running under the back of preceding stitches, to begin and end threads, causes those stitches to be pulled tighter on the front of the ground fabric. Even when a smaller needle is used to anchor, placing the ending thread under the back of stitches will disturb the tension on the front of the work. The practice of running under stitches can force carefully stitched threads to be disturbed.

◆ An alternate way to start or end a thread is with a 'L' stitch. Make a tiny stitch over one canvas thread (if working on canvas) or slightly less than $1/_8$" long on fabric. Go through to the back of the ground. Come back up about $1/_8$", or one canvas thread, away from the first stitch. Make a second tiny stitch that ends in the same place as the first stitch. Thus, a small 'L.' Try to pierce the thread of the first stitch with the second stitch as it enters the ground. This adds additional security to the anchor. The same procedure can be used to end a thread.

A COMPLETED
'L' STITCH

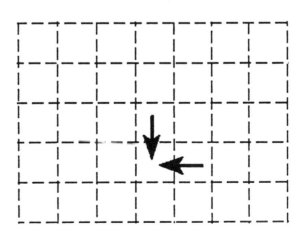

To begin with an L stitch: Make a small knot in the end of the thread. Cut off any tail which extends beyond the knot. Come up from the back of the fabric within the area to be stitched. Make an L stitch. The knot will remain on the back of the work. Such a small knot will not show after embroidery is finished.

To end with an L stitch: Use the same two small stitches, forming an L, to end your thread. Part the embroidery in a stitched section and bring needle up from back. Make first small stitch and go through to back. Do second stitch. Bring thread back to front the third time, and clip off very close to surface of fabric. The stitching will fall back on top, and hide, the L stitch. When ending, greater security is achieved by making two L stitches in a stitched section. Then clip thread.

◆   If you are ending very slippery threads, there is an alternate way to anchor. In this case, on the back of the work, run under three or four near-by stitches, bring the needle out, take a small back stitch over the last stitch run under, and then slide under two or three more stitches. Note that this is all done on the back of the work, the back of the ground fabric, and the back of the stitching. This little extra anchor is called a 'bargello tuck.' You may want to do more than one tuck.

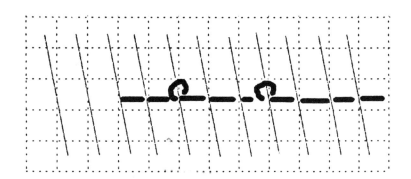

BARGELLO TUCK

◆   Bargello tucks require that you run under stitches, which can disturb the front of the stitched area. When forced to do this, do not pass the

needle under the entire stitch backing. Rather, skim through the underside of the stitches, actually splitting the back of the stitching threads. There is still some change in tension on the front of the stitch, but it will be minimized.

◆   Always try to anchor under areas which are worked in the same color as the thread being ended/begun. If this is totally impossible, be sure to end under stitches worked in the same value thread.

In other words, do not end purple thread under the back of a section worked in yellow. It will almost certainly cause a shadow from the front. Also, do not end the yellow under purple stitches. This can cause light colored flecks to show on the front. End purple under dark sections, yellow under light areas.

◆   As a general rule, ending and beginning tails should be placed in the direction in which the stitch is worked. Thus, if you work the stitch horizontally, place the ending/beginning anchor on the horizontal.

The exception to this, and a very important exception, is diagonal tent stitch (basketweave). Although diagonal tent is worked on the diagonal, always place beginning and ending anchors on *either* the horizontal or vertical line of the canvas.

Within an area of diagonal tent stitch, be consistent in placing the anchors all horizontally or all vertically on the canvas. If you place anchors so that they are on the diagonal, the addition of the extra tension on the back of the stitches will increase the diagonal stripe of the stitch on the front. If both horizontal and vertical anchors are used within a section, a double thickness of thread where the horizontal and vertical, beginning or ending, threads cross will create bumps on the surface of the work.

◆   A *pin*, or *pin head*, stitch is a tiny stitch used to secure the direction of the thread. Another name for a pin stitch might be 'tacking stitch.' For

example, if you must change the angle from which the working thread travels, fasten the thread with a pin stitch before continuing to work. Or, to preserve the angle of stitches when moving from one row to the next, secure the thread with a pin stitch. On canvas a pin stitch will go over one canvas thread. On fabric, it should be about $\frac{1}{8}$" long. A pin stitch is actually one-half of an L stitch.

A pin stitch works well when doing pulled work. It helps to stabilize the working thread and gives the first pulled stitch the same appearance as the other stitches. The pin stitch will be hidden by the stitch which covers it.

PIN STITCH AS USED IN PULLED WORK

PIN STITCH IS
#1-#2

FIRST REGULAR
STITCH IS
#3- #4

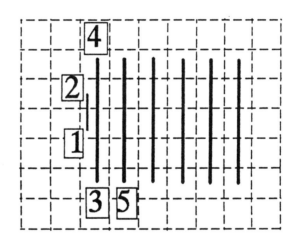

◆ If you are working on linen, or similar closely woven ground fabric, which has been placed on a stretcher-strip type working frame, be especially careful of the edges. The area where the fabric wraps around the frame is very prone to soiling which is difficult to remove. Try covering the edges with cotton strips tacked in place. Or, there are commercial frame covers which go over the edges of the stretcher frame. Find these in needlework shops.

◆ "Always" work particular stitches the same way. For instance, always make the top half of a cross stitch from lower left to upper right;

always do dove's eyes in a clockwise direction, square fillets counter-clockwise. Or, whatever ways work best for you. You will be less apt to make a mistake if you make a habit of doing such stitches the same way. In this case, "Always" might not be every time. The method might have to be altered to accommodate design requirements.

◆   When doing a long row of basting on evenweave fabric, put in a 'counter.' The basting stitches should go over and under the same number threads. A good number is four. Every given number of threads, do a small stitch perpendicular to the basting line. Thus, baste over and under every four ground threads. At the same time, every twenty threads, or five groups of four, do a perpendicular stitch. When you check how many threads have been basted, is easier to count the perpendiculars rather than individual groups of four. Adjust the number of ground threads covered by the basting stitches, and the interval of perpendiculars, as needed by the length of the line.

PHOTOCOPY OF
BASTING SHOWING
COUNTER STITCHES

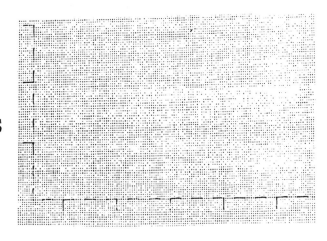

◆   When doing canvas work, *never* count canvas holes. Count the canvas threads as you work stitches. Counting holes will result in a stitch which is not the desired, or expected, size.

◆   It is a basic rule of canvas work: whenever possible come up in an empty hole, go down in a filled hole. You can see where the needle is going when you go down into a hole. If there is already a thread in

that hole, you will be less likely to snag it if you can see where you are placing your needle.

◆ In almost every embroidery technique, diagonal stitches offer better coverage of the ground fabric than straight stitches, even though they are worked with the same number strands in the needle. This is especially true in canvas work. It is a common practice to do straight stitches with one strand more than is used for diagonal stitches.

Be sure to experiment with the proposed stitch, outside the design, near the edge of the ground or on a doodle cloth. By trying a different number strands, you can determine which offers the best effect for the design.

◆ Stitch those objects which are on 'top,' or in the foreground, first. Then stitch those which are to the back. The 'back' objects can be worked so that they come up to the edges of the front items. If you stitch the back objects first, you are left with just an unworked area on the ground, into which you must fit the foreground objects.

◆ Do not permit 'carry threads' on the reverse side of your needlework. These are the threads which travel from one working area to another. If the section between the two areas is not worked, and sometimes even if it is, those carry threads can shadow through to the front. Such shadows are unsightly and can ruin an otherwise excellent piece of needlework.

◆ It is best not to jump from one section to another with the same working thread. Not only could carry thread shadows be created, but the stitch angle will change.

If the stitch you are doing is worked from left to right, and each one begins at the bottom, you must maintain that progression. If you jump from another section and the working thread comes from the top right,

rather than upper left, this difference will show in the altered angle of that first stitch. The same is true whenever stitch progression is varied.

◆ The thread that travels from one stitch unit to the next will often show through to the front if you are doing open work on a loosely woven fabric. An example might be blackwork done with red thread on white needlepoint canvas. To hide these traveling threads, use a piece of closely woven fabric such muslin, or even a light weight interfacing.

Baste the ground and extra fabric together, with the ground on top and the basting around the outer edges. If you are working on a large design, it may make your work easier to baste lines across the face of the work. Remove basting as the embroidery secures the two fabrics together.

Stitch the embroidery through the ground and extra backing fabric. It possibly will be necessary to use a sharp needle to pierce the closely woven fabric. This piece of backing fabric will hide the traveling threads between stitch units.

◆ If you run out of thread when doing an on-going stitch such as chain, try this. Work until the needle is at the back of the work, but do not pull the last loop tight. Put the old thread to one side. With a second needle and new thread, begin with a running anchor in the unworked section, about one inch ahead of where the old thread ended. Bring the new thread up in the place where the old thread would have come, had you been able to continue stitching with it. Do a couple of stitches with the new thread. Then pull the last loop made by the old thread, tight. Again put old thread to one side. Stitch until the running anchor is covered and clip the knot. End the old thread by anchoring under preceding stitching. Instructions for a running anchor are elsewhere in this Technique section.

◆ As you stitch, you twist the needle. After several stitches, the working thread is either overly twisted or untwisted. It has to do with the

direction you twist as you stitch. Also, the yarn or thread in the eye of the needle moves, while the needle itself is still in your fingers. Every few stitches, twirl the needle between your thumb and forefinger. This will correct the twist put in the thread as you stitched. After a short time, twirling the needle will become an unconscious habit.

◆ An alternate method of removing the twist put in the thread as it is stitched, is to allow the threaded needle to dangle free from the work. The thread will untwist as it hangs. While this method is certainly effective, it also interferes with the flow of stitching. Most experienced stitchers prefer to twirl the needle every few stitches, thus correcting the twist.

◆ Tension is very important to the final appearance of any stitches. The *consistency* of that tension is vital. A piece which is worked with stitches that are *all* too tight is better than one with some stitches too tight, others too loose, and still others with correct tension. Certainly it is best to have all stitches of correct tension, and stitchers should practice to reach that goal. Through repetition comes excellence.

◆ Proper tension is determined by the technique and stitch being worked. For instance, the strong tension used for many pulled thread stitches would not be appropriate for surface embroidery on silk ground fabric. A good instruction book will help by describing and illustrating correct tension, however nothing can replace classroom participation with a qualified teacher for help with stitch tension and advice.

◆ Do not try to change stitch tension when working on a piece that you expect to be handed down for generations. All embroiderers want their best work to be on such a design. Therefore, be especially aware of tension when working on less important pieces or notebook samples. Soon, correct tension will become automatic and such skill will be evident on heirloom work.

◆ When you come to the edge of a section, but have only worked part of a stitch unit, you must *compensate*. To compensate is to do the best you can with what you have; to do as much of the stitch unit as there is area available.

Put the point of the needle where the stitch, or part of the stitch, should end, even though it is outside the edge of the design. Do not put the needle into the ground. Maintaining the slant, or direction, of this stitch stroke, drag the needle backwards until you reach the design boundary. Do not permit the point of the needle to mar the ground. Then insert into ground material. Proceed with the balance of the compensated stitch unit.

◆ An alternate method to determine how to compensate a stitch unit requires a piece of graph paper. Draw the complete stitch on the graph. Then, with another piece of paper, cover that part which will be beyond the edge of the area. What is showing is the section which will fit. This procedure works especially well for counted thread work, but with a bit of visual concentration, is also good for other forms of embroidery.

◆ Knotted stitches such as French knot, coral, or buttonhole, should always be pulled in a consistent direction. Problems could arise if you work a coral stitch with some knots tightened by pulling to the left and some by pulling to the right. The knots will have an inconsistent appearance. They could also loosen and become sloppy.

◆ A tent stitch is a small stitch which covers a single canvas mesh from lower left to upper right. It is considered the basic stitch of canvas work. A group or section of these is also called tent stitch, as opposed to tent stitch_es_. One would say, "That entire design is worked in tent stitch," not "That entire design is worked in tent stitch_es_."

There are three methods of working tent stitch. They have approximately the same appearance on the front, but very different on the

back. The following is a brief description of each stitch. A canvas work stitch book will give more explicit directions for working each of them.

HALF CROSS STITCH is worked in horizontal rows from left to right. At the end of the each row, the canvas is inverted to work the next. The needle comes up at the lower left of the mesh to be covered, and enters the canvas at the upper right. On the back, the working thread travels vertically down to begin the next stitch unit to the right.

Half cross stitch badly warps the canvas. Its lack of backing makes it a poor choice for any item which will receive wear.

CONTINENTAL STITCH is worked in horizontal rows from right to left. The needle emerges from the back of the canvas at the lower left of the mesh, and enters at the top right. On the back, the working thread travels on a long diagonal from the top of one stitch to the lower left of the next unit to the left. At the end of a row, the canvas may be inverted to work the next. Or, the next row may be worked by reversing the procedure bringing the needle up in the base of the stitches of the first row.

Continental may also be worked vertically and to both diagonals. It is excellent for single rows of tent stitch or very tiny areas. A major weakness of the stitch is that areas of continental badly warp the canvas. Such warping is especially evident if the stitched area is large.

In the past, areas of tent stitch were frequently done in a combination of continental and half cross. A row of continental was worked from right to left. Then a row of half cross was stitched from left to right. Using this method the stitcher did not have to invert the canvas every other row. Since there is a slight difference in the appearance on the front of these two stitches, the practice forms very inconsistent stitches. This method should be avoided.

DIAGONAL TENT or BASKETWEAVE is worked in diagonal rows. The needle comes up from the back at the lower left of the mesh and enters at the upper right. On the back, the working thread travels either up or down to the lower left of the next mesh on the straight diagonal. A basketweave pattern is formed on the back of the canvas as rows are worked up and then down. The back traveling thread changes direction. On rows worked upwards, the travel thread is horizontal. On rows stitched downward, the travel thread is vertical. Because of the alternate tension of the horizontal and vertical travel threads, the stitch does not distort the canvas. Diagonal tent is generally the stitch of choice when more than a single line of tent stitch is needed.

◆ Gross point and petit point refer to the size of tent stitches in canvas work. Gross point are those stitches which are larger than eighteen per inch. Petit point are those stitches which are eighteen per inch, or smaller.

Since a tent stitch is worked over a single canvas mesh, the terms gross point and petit point are also frequently used to describe the canvas size. Thus, petit point canvas would be one with more than eighteen threads per inch.

◆ Diagonal tent, or basketweave, should be stitched with the grain of the canvas. Work the rows going *up* over mesh which have a horizontal canvas thread on top of the intersection of the canvas threads. *Down* rows should be stitched over mesh which have a vertical thread on top.

To help minimize the diagonal stripe created by this stitch, always follow a row worked upwards with one which is worked down. Some embroiderers will never end a thread at the top or bottom of a row. They are afraid they will forget in which direction the next row should be stitched. They will only stop when in the middle of a row. Then, when they start again, they will be certain to continue the pattern of up and down rows. If you work up rows where horizontal threads are on

top, and down rows over vertical top threads, you will not have to end your working thread in the middle of a row.

◆   When doing canvas work, the point where a section worked in a diagonal stitch meets one worked in a straight stitch, often gives embroiderers a problem. The straight and diagonal stitches should overlap. Work the diagonals so that they cover the mesh which are along one side of the canvas channel in which the straight stitches are worked. If this overlapping technique is not followed, canvas threads will be left exposed.

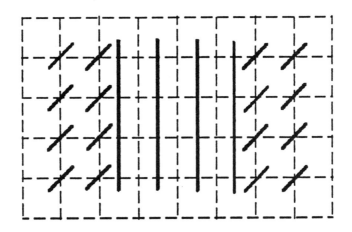

DIAGONAL STITCHES NEXT TO VERTICAL STITCHES

◆   An excellent way to check any evenweave work for missing stitches is to hold the piece up to a strong light, that from a window works well. Strong daylight coming through will accent any missing stitches.

◆   When cutting threads for hardanger work, always be sure your scissors are to the left of the kloster block. This makes for a cleaner cut and fewer ground fabric 'nubs' showing. The same is true when cutting threads for drawn fabric work on canvas or other evenweave material.

The next several pages contain information on how to lay stranded threads. The first pages are a narrative description. Following that are several pages of screened photos. The laying tool depicted in these photos is a collar stay because it is easier to see it in photographs than a thin, pointed laying tool. The process is the same whichever laying tool you use.

Laying stranded threads is described as it is done on canvas. The technique is the same for laying threads on any ground material.

Additional information on laying tools and working frames can be found in the Implements section.

Additional information on beginning and ending threads with the waste knot method can be found in the Techniques section.

HOW TO LAY STRANDED THREADS

USE A WORKING FRAME OR HOOP, FABRIC SHOULD BE
TIGHTLY STRETCHED TO PRESENT A FIRM
FOUNDATION FOR LAYING THE THREAD

USE A LAYING TOOL SUCH AS BODKIN, COLLAR STAY,
LARGE NEEDLE, TEKOBARI, OR OTHER SPECIAL ITEM
TO ALIGN STRANDS

'STRIP' THREADS

THREAD NEEDLE WITH CORRECT NUMBER STRANDS FOR
DESIRED COVERAGE

Start with threaded needle at the top of canvas (after forming waste knot), where you wish to begin the first stitch. Grasp needle with thumb and first finger of the non-dominant, or upper, hand. In the remaining three fingers of this top hand you should be holding your laying tool. Put the needle into the canvas where the stitch is to end.

Take hold of the needle with your bottom, or dominant, hand. Pull thread part way through canvas.

From the top, while drawing the thread through the canvas, move the laying tool from the three fingers to between the thumb and first finger, and place it under the thread that is entering the canvas. As the thread is pulled gently to the back and thus over the laying tool, stroke the thread with the laying tool several times. The laying tool should be stroked from the base of the stitch toward where it enters the canvas. This will cause the strands to straighten. The stroking motion should be done while there is just enough thread still on top of the canvas to form some slack. Thus the laying tool will be able to straighten the strands.

Once the strands are straight over the laying tool, allow the thread to come to rest against the canvas by pulling it gently from the underside. Hold the stitch down with the point or side of the laying tool. With lower hand put tip of needle back up through canvas where next stitch is to start. Place first or second finger of lower hand against thread where it emerges at end of first stitch on underside of canvas. Hold this stitch with lower hand until thread is completely through to front of canvas. Grasp needle with top hand and pull thread to front of canvas. Repeat operation for each stitch.

The beauty of your work depends on how well you lay the threads. It is more difficult to describe this operation than to perform it.

THE PHOTOGRAPHS ON THE NEXT PAGES ILLUSTRATE THE CORRECT TECHNIQUE FOR LAYING STRANDED THREADS.

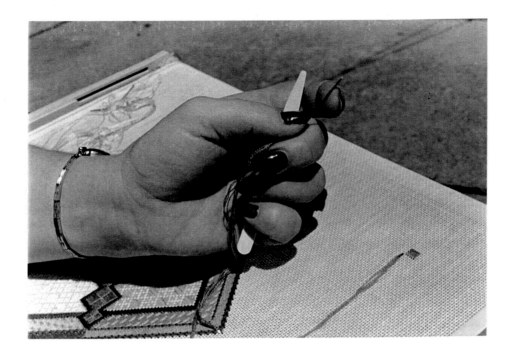

1. Grasp needle with thumb and first finger of upper (non-dominate) hand. Laying tool is held by remaining three fingers. Pointed end of laying tool will be in the 'circle' formed by thumb and first finger.

2. Insert needle into canvas, still holding laying tool, but helping to guide needle with second finger.

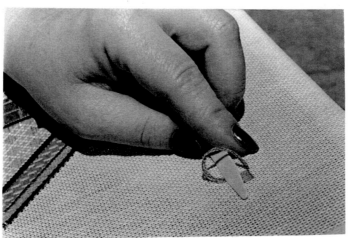

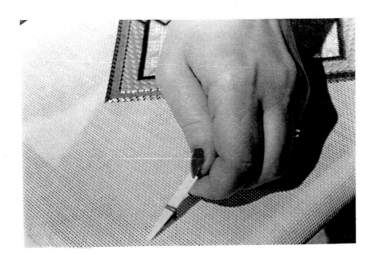

3. Move laying tool to between thumb and first two fingers. Place the tool under thread that is entering canvas. Stroke thread with the laying tool from where it exits the canvas, over the laying tool, and to where it enters the canvas at the end of the stitch. Repeat stroking motion, if necessary, but be sure to maintain the same direction as above—from base of stitch to where it enters material.

4. Hold stitch down against top of canvas with point or side of laying tool.

5. With lower hand, put tip of needle back up through canvas where next stitch is to begin.

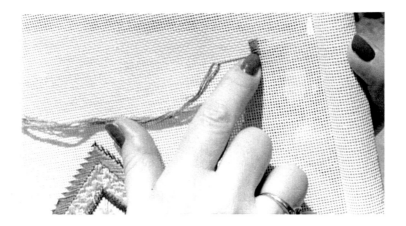

6. Place first or second finger of lower hand against underside of stitch to hold in place as thread is drawn to top of canvas.

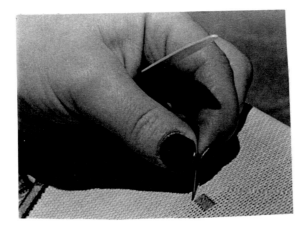

7. Continuing to hold stitch from under side, grasp needle with upper hand and pull thread to front of canvas ready to begin next stitch. Repeat for succeeding stitches.

A BIT ABOUT DESIGN AND EMBROIDERY

◆ Many embroiderers consider design and color theory to be dry and dull. However, just a basic knowledge of these can help you when purchasing a chart, a painted canvas, a kit, when making minor or major changes in any of these, or when creating a design of your own. If you have this fundamental understanding, your finished work will be more appealing. It only makes good sense to spend your time and money for materials on a project that is a good design.

◆ Consider the Elements of Design as the building blocks. In basic terms and with short descriptions, the Elements of Design are:

> LINE A mark longer than it is wide. It may be an actual line drawn or stitched on the ground, such as a flower stem. Or, it may be an implied line such as a horizon.

> SHAPE A series of lines, or a single line, of different directions, which enclose an area.

> FORM A shape which has, or appears to have, dimension and contour.

> COLOR or HUE That sensation, perceived by the eye, which is caused by light rays reflected back from a surface.

> TEXTURE The quality of a surface which causes it to be, or appear to be, rough, smooth, bumpy, flat, etc.

◆ Think of the Principles of Design as the tools which are applied to the Elements of Design. Again using very simple terms and short definitions, the Principles of Design are:

> BALANCE The sense of stability between visually opposing attractions.

MOVEMENT A path the eye follows when viewing a design.

REPETITION or RHYTHM Somewhat similar components duplicated at regular, or irregular, intervals.

EMPHASIS or DOMINANCE The area of major interest.

CONTRAST Difference, such as warm or cool, light or dark, rough or smooth, large or small.

◆   UNITY is achieved when a harmonious and pleasing composition is created.

◆   The Elements of Design are manipulated by the Principles of Design to achieve Unity. The elements are the objects or subjects; the principles are the actions we apply to those objects. The organization of the elements, according to the principles, creates harmony. If we select the elements, and use the principles, carefully, we create the basis for a good embroidery.

◆   Continuing to use basic terms, the types of design forms are:

GEOMETRIC Uses shapes such as squares, circles, or angles.

GRAPHIC Includes letters or numbers. In embroidery, examples of graphic design are samplers.

ABSTRACT Must represent something with form, such as a building, flower, or person. An abstract generally does not represent an idea or concept unless it does so with one or more forms.

NON-OBJECTIVE Does not represent anything. The portrayal is totally from the imagination of the designer. Frequently the image illustrates an idea or concept.

REPEAT PATTERNS One or more established patterns which are duplicated many times over. In embroidery, examples of repeat patterns are diaper and blackwork patterns.

♦ Smooth or shiny textures are stronger than those which are rough or dull.

♦ The upper left area of a composition is supposedly stronger than any other section. Thus, the lower right section is the weakest. While this is subject to opinion, and will be affected by the specific design, the concept is worth considering.

♦ Diagonal stitches are perceived by most to be more graceful than vertical or horizontal stitches.

♦ Diagonal lines create movement within a design and can be characterized as emotional.

♦ Vertical lines, whether it be an actual line or the implication of one, are dramatic and strong.

♦ Horizontal lines are somewhat weaker, and more restful.

♦ Because a stitch is worked in a given direction, it does not follow that the appearance of the finished area will have the same direction. Thus a stitch worked in horizontal rows may have a vertical, or diagonal, appearance when the section is completed.

♦ Large shapes seem to come forward. Small shapes recede.

◆   Shapes which touch convey tension. Overlapping shapes give the illusion of more than one level.

◆   *Positive space* is that which is occupied by an object. *Negative space* is the background between objects in a composition. Never under-estimate the importance of negative space. It should enhance the composition. For example, too much negative space can cause a design to be over powered by the background. Too much positive space gives the eye no place to rest within a composition. The piece gives the appearance of being 'busy.'

◆   It is not necessary to put the center of interest, or focal point, in the center of a design. In many cases, the composition will be improved if the main area of interest is off-center. Each design should dictate the location of the central focus.

◆   The highlights created by shiny metallics and metals will make those sections appear dominate. A small metallic area is equal in importance to a much larger area worked in a thread which is has a duller finish.

A BIT ABOUT COLOR AND EMBROIDERY

◆ Color is the most influential element used in embroidery. The selection of colors sets the emotional tone of a composition.

◆ The human eye sees colors as mixtures. This phenomenon is called optical mixing. An embroiderer cannot mix colors as paints are mixed. However, the needleartist can combine colors in the needle to approximate the results achieved by mixing paints.

Optical mixing does not always mean that yellow and blue threads mixed in the needle will make clear green stitches. Depending on which colors and values are used, a very grayed green may be formed. It is most important to experiment.

◆ Without going into overly technical terms, the four attributes, or characteristics, of color are:

HUE is the name of the color, such as red, yellow, blue. Hue is often used interchangeably with the word *color*.

TEMPERATURE refers to whether a color is warm or cool. Warm colors are associated with fire, the cool colors with water. Red, yellow, and orange are warm. Blue, green and violet are cool. Cool colors can be made warm_er_ and warm colors can be made cool_er_. For instance, red violet is warmer than violet or blue-violet because of the addition of the red. Blue-green is cooler than green or yellow-green because of the addition of the cool blue.

VALUE is the relative lightness or darkness of a color.

INTENSITY refers to the purity or saturation of a color. An intense color has nothing added to it. For instance, pure red is a fully saturated, or intense, color. If you add white to it, creating pink, the intensity of the red has been breached.

◆   Warm colors tend to attract greater attention than cool colors.

◆   A *gray scale* measures the value of a color. A gray scale is a strip of paints or color chips. Black is at one end, white at the other. There can be an infinite number of grays in between. Black is 100% value, white is 0% value. The middle gray is 50% value.

Although a gray scale can be any size you would like it to be, a common sized one will be approximately an inch wide and about ten inches long. It will be divided into nine positions. The sections will be black and white at either end and seven values of gray will be shaded between them. This is large enough so that you can determine the value of a thread.

You may make a gray scale with paints or color chips. You may also purchase one in almost any art supply store.

Use the gray scale to determine the value of a thread. Hold the thread against the gray scale. Squint your eyes until all ambient room light is eliminated. Move the color up and down the gray scale until the it appears to 'match' one of the grays. Such a match indicates the value of that color.

◆   A *value scale* is created using a color. A very dark shade of the color will be at one end, a very light tint at the other. In between will be the values as they correspond to those on a gray scale. The pure hue, with no white or black added, will be in the middle position.

◆   A composition that has all of its colors in the same value will appear flat. Interest is created by varying, not just the colors used in a design, but also their values.

◆   Make a photocopy of your design. Do a black and white copy rather than a color copy. This photocopy will allow you to see where the

various values are located in your needlework. You can check to be certain you have varied the values within the project.

By photocopying just threads, you can see what value they are. Considering thread value before it is stitched can help you determine the placement of various values.

◆   A *tint* is a color to which white has been added. For example, the tint of red is pink.

◆   A *shade* is a color to which black has been added. A shade of red is maroon. Some experts define shade as a color combined with the color across the color wheel from it. Or, the color with the addition of its compliment.

◆   A *tone* is a color to which gray has been added. An example of a grayed red is the value associated with colonial reds. Gray can be added to a tint. For example, gray can be added to pink which is a tint of red.

◆   *Tints*, *tones*, and *shades* are values and intensities of a color. A shade is closer to black on the gray scale than is a tint. Tints, tones, and shades are not fully saturated, or intense, colors because they have had either white, black, or gray added to the pure hue.

◆   A *color wheel*, or *hue circle*, is an arrangement of colors in a circle. A frequently used color wheel has twelve positions.

The *primary* colors are red, yellow, and blue. They are located on the color wheel as if they were at the points of an equilateral triangle (all three sides of equal length) placed inside the wheel.

The *secondary* colors are created by mixing two adjacent primary colors together. They are green (yellow + blue), orange (red + yellow), and violet (red + blue). Each of these colors fit on the color wheel, between the two primaries from which it is formed.

The *intermediate* colors (intermediaries) result from mixing a primary color with the secondary next to it. Thus, red and orange make red-orange. Each of these fit into the wheel between their primary and secondary components.

◆ Not found on a twelve point color wheel are the *tertiary* colors (tertiaries). They are, however, very important colors. Tertiary colors result from the mixture of two secondaries. Orange and violet become russet, violet and green are slate, and green and orange, olive.

◆ It is not necessary to make your own color wheel, unless you so desire. Printed wheels are sold at art supply stores. They come in a wide range of prices and some are relatively inexpensive. Be certain to compare all the color wheels available. The printed colors may be off to varying degrees. Let your eyes and color perception be your guide in deciding which to purchase.

◆ Basic color schemes are helpful when deciding on colors for an embroidery. A *color scheme*, or *color harmony*, may use not just the pure colors listed, but any of the tints, tones, and shades of those colors.

When determining which colors fit into a scheme, it may be helpful to have a color wheel available. The basic color schemes are:

Black and white which includes any of the values of gray between the two extremes. Some color authorities say that a small amount of a single value of one color may be included in this harmony. Thus, a black and white color scheme might include

black, gray, and white, with a small accent area of red, or other color.

Complementary consists of colors across from each other on the color wheel. A complementary scheme of red and green might also include pink and dark forest green.

Split complementary is one color plus the two on either side of its complement.

Double spilt complement consists of the two colors on each side of two complements. The complements themselves are not part of this color scheme.

Analogous is composed of colors which are adjacent on the color wheel. Some authorities say that these must be limited to three colors. Others say that as many as six adjacent colors can comprise an analogous scheme. Compositions which use fewer analogous colors, three or four, are stronger than those which use many colors.

Triadic schemes are determined by putting a triangle inside the color wheel. The points of the triangle indicate which three colors should be included. Some authorities insist that an equilateral triangle (all three sides of equal length) be used to determine the three colors. Others theorize that an isosceles triangle (two of the three sides are of equal length) may also be used.

Monochromatic consists of the tints, tones, and shades of one color. As with the black and white color scheme, some authorities tell us that a monochromatic color scheme may also have a small area of an accent color.

Multicolor schemes are those which do not have a discernable classification. Construction of multicolor schemes must be approached with great care in order to avoid the appearance of chaos.

◆ A color, or shape, appears lighter if it is placed on a dark background. Conversely, a color appears darker if placed on a light background.

◆ Dark colors, or shapes, will come forward when placed on a light background. Light shapes and colors will come forward on a dark background.

◆ A small area of color will appear darker. A large area of a color will appear lighter.

◆ If equal parts of complimentary colors, of the same intensity, are mixed, they will create gray. While embroiderers do not mix colors as painters do, it is important to remember this when mixing colors in the needle. Stitching with one strand of red plus one strand of green, of the same intensity, in the needle, will force the eye to see a grayed area.

◆ A *small* amount of its compliment will strengthen a color. For instance, nothing makes the leaves of a tree look greener than a few tiny areas of red.

◆ A composition, in any color scheme, which has equal amounts of several colors, will generally be dull and boring. Use unequal areas of each color. Interest will also be heightened by varying the intensity of those colors.

◆ Because color is composed of light, technically the presence of all colors is white. The absence of color is black.

◆ *Simultaneous contrast* involves what is known as 'after image.' The classic demonstration of simultaneous contrast is to stare at a 3″ or 4″

square of bright red for about thirty seconds. Then immediately look at a white surface. Your eyes will seem to manufacture the complement of red, and cause the white to appear green.

In basic terms, the eye attempts to achieve a neutral, and in that effort will produce a color's complement. The same concept is true with light and dark. When we look at a bright light, then shift to normal lighting, we see dark images.

◆   It is not necessary to always be aware of the technical explanation of simultaneous contrast. It is very important to remember that each color in a composition is affected by all others in the same work.

◆   There are four basic types of shading. These are accomplished by various methods in needlework.

> *Stylized* shading is the outlining of an object in a darker value of the same color, or in a strong contrasting color.

> *Ombre* shading graduates from light to dark, or dark to light. The change is gradual, row by row or section by section, from one color to another.

> *Realistic* shading, also known as traditional, or soft shading, creates the look of realism. It is frequently considered the most difficult to achieve.

> *Pointillistic* shading, which in embroidery is often referred to as scatter shading, uses dots of color. These dots, or stitches, are strategically placed, just as in the pointillism method of painting.

◆   Try to select colors for a design in the same type of light in which the finished object will be viewed. Artificial lighting, especially that which needlework shops may be forced to used, drastically changes colors. If the project is going to be displayed under artificial lighting, choose

colors in that same type of artificial light. If it is to be in a location where there is natural light, choose colors in daylight.

◆ In a hank or skein, thread will appear stronger and more intense in color than it will when it is stitched. Tiny shadows cast by small stitches will make the color seem slightly darker. Areas worked in long straight stitches will seem lighter in color than those done in small stitches, even though they are worked in the same color and value.

◆ Highly textured stitches appear darker than those with less texture.

◆ If you cannot decide what color ground fabric to use, consider the following. As a rule of thumb, white fabric is for designs which use primary colors. Other designs will look best on ivory or a colored fabric. This assumes that the ground material will provide the background color.

OTHER THINGS

♦   Use bubble wrap to protect embroidery pieces when you have to ship them. Place tissue paper, preferably acid free tissue, next to the embroidery surface, then wrap in the plastic bubbles. Put in a plastic bag, to protect from water damage, and then pack in a strong cardboard box.

From a conservation point of view, it is best to avoid contact between embroidery and plastic. On the other hand, very possibly it is worse to have your embroidery rain soaked in a soggy box. The tissue will keep the plastic from touching the embroidery.

♦   If you ever need to keep track of how long you work on an embroidery, there is an easy way. Use an electric clock. Set it at 12:00. Then plug it in while you work, unplug it when you stop. The only thing you will have to check is how often the clock passes 12:00.

♦   In common usage, canvas work, canvas embroidery, and needlepoint are all names for the same type of needlework.

♦   An *ort* is a scrap of thread. The pieces you throw away because they are too short for stitching. An *ort bag* is a small bag to collect orts so that they do not litter your stitching area.

♦   When you finishing a stitching session, leave your needle threaded. Starting with a threaded needle helps you get back into the stitching rhythm, faster, the next time you work.

◆ When ripping, try a pair of scissors that are somewhat dull at the points. You will be less likely to cut the ground fabric.

◆ Always make sure that the points of the scissors are pointing *up* when you are ripping stitches. Slip them under the stitches to be cut, then raise the points. You should be able to see the tips above the stitches to be cut. If you can see them, they will not be cutting your ground fabric or something else you really do not want to cut.

◆ Some people like to use a seam ripper to remove stitches. Others say that seam rippers are too sharp. There are items on the market designed just to cut stitches. They make ripping easier for some stitchers. Which you use is a matter of personal opinion. Each embroiderer must decide for themselves.

◆ Why are two seemingly identical threads, or fabrics, very different prices? Especially if one is quite a bit more expensive than the other? Other than an item being on sale, it is frequently a difference in quality. Perhaps the less expensive item has more sizing to make it feel heavier. This is not *always* the case, but as usual, you generally get what you pay for. Your time to do the embroidery will be about the same whether you use good or poor quality materials, so it is wise to stitch with the best you can afford. Many times the better quality thread is easier to stitch with.

◆ Whether you work your design on a frame, or 'in hand,' depends on the technique. If you are working on a frame, you must use the 'stabbing' method of stitching. That is, put the needle down into the fabric, pull it, and the thread, all the way through to the back. Push needle up from back, pull all the way through to the front.

If working in hand, you may use a 'sewing' motion. Take a small bite of fabric, passing the <u>point</u> of the needle from the front of the fabric to the underside, then back to the top and pull thread through.

◆ To determine the finished size of a chart on a given piece of even-weave ground fabric, divide the number of charted stitches by the size of the ground. If the chart has 168 stitches, and you wish to work it on 14 count fabric, the finished size would be 12 inches (168 divided by 14). This assumes that each stitch is over one intersection of horizontal and vertical ground threads.

◆ To determine the amount of thread needed to work an area of a specific stitch, do a one square inch sample of the stitch, on the ground to be used for the design, with the intended thread. Keep track of the amount of thread used. Multiply by the number of square inches in the proposed section.

Remember to take into consideration the number of plies or strands you will use when doing the mathematics. Assume that the thread comes with seven plies per strand, you used one ply in your needle, and it took two plies to stitch a square inch. When you do the figuring, remember that using all of the entire strand will cover three and one half times the area than will just two plies.

◆ If you have many colors or threads started on the same piece, draw each to the front of the ground fabric, when it is not being used. Only have one working thread at the back of the work at one time. When many threads are left to dangle on the back, there is the potential for massive tangles.

◆ When working an area and you run out of room before you finish a full stitch unit, you must *compensate*. That is, you will do the best you can — work as much of the stitch or stitch pattern as the available space allows.

If you are having trouble figuring how much of a stitch you can do, it helps to draw the stitch on a piece of graph paper. Use another piece

of paper and cover that section of the stitch that would be beyond the edge of the area. What is left then, is what you can work.

Most important is that the compensated part of the stitch should not attract attention. It should appear to be part of the pattern.

◆ Protect work-in-progress with a washed cotton pillow case, or similar covering, while you are not working on it. If you are not concerned about plastic touching your design, you can use a plastic bag. Do protect your needlework from dust and dirt with some form of covering.

◆ Never 'park' needles through the ground fabric, within the design area. In other words, never take a bite of the ground with your needle, and then leave the needle there for a period of time. A needle which is left in the fabric will distort the threads of the ground. Such distortion can easily be seen on needlepoint canvas, and will also cause holes in more closely woven materials. Needles which have been left within the design area possibly will cause rust or black marks that will permanently stain the fabric.

◆ When you are temporarily away from stitching a piece, such as overnight or when you are away from home during the day, do not forget to put the work some place where it is safe from puppies, kittens and children. They all love to tangle those long threads. Many pieces of needlework have been ruined by curious kittens.

◆ Remember that food, drink and needlework <u>NEVER</u>, **NEVER** mix. This is especially true when taking a class. You certainly would not want to have your coffee spill, spoiling someone's work. And, you would not want their food to stain your embroidery.

◆ An embroidery worked with silk should be dry cleaned. Even if the threads test colorfast in water, submersion may prove too much for the dyes.

◆ If there is any rayon thread in an embroidery, plan on having it dry cleaned, rather than washed. Rayon will permanently wrinkle when wet with water.

◆ Plastic canvas cannot be dry cleaned. The solvents will dissolve the grid. Items made of plastic canvas, and items which have plastic canvas used as a stiffener or stabilizer, should be hand washed.

◆ When looking for a dry cleaner to trust cleaning needlework, the best source of information is likely to be other stitchers your area. It is also wise to talk with a representative of the establishment to determine the extent of their experience with the embroidery being considered. Be certain to tell the cleaners exactly what the ground material and threads are made of.

◆ Yarns and threads sold today have been mothproofed, if appropriate, by the manufacturer. It is not necessary to use additional mothproofing chemicals. Such extra chemicals can cause color bleeding which might not occur in usual colorfast tests.

◆ Be very careful of dirt protection sprays. These sprays are supposed to keep stains from becoming permanent. However, the chemicals used in them frequently interact with thread or ground fabric dyes, or with markers/paints used to put a design on the fabric. Bleeding often results. Test any protection spray on scrap fabric, threads, and markers before using it on your finished embroidery.

Dirt and stain protection treatments have not been available long enough to evaluate their effect on embroidery materials. Use on pieces of heirloom quality should be avoided.

◆   Stitched needlepoint canvas can be washed, if necessary, assuming that the threads used for the embroidery can also be washed. Be prepared to loose some canvas sizing.

◆   No matter how careful we are, stains on needlework do happen. Handle the problem as soon as possible. The longer a stain remains, the more permanent it becomes. The following are a few common stains with suggestions on how they possibly can be removed. Washing is noted in several instances. Do consider the materials involved and have the piece dry cleaned if more appropriate. If you wash the piece, be very certain that you rinse it until all soap is completely removed.

Commercial pre-wash sprays or sticks perhaps will be effective for these stains, also. Since the following are less caustic than the commercial products, you possibly will want to try them first.

BLOOD   Apply the saliva of the person who made the blood stain. Then wash, if applicable.

COFFEE or TEA   Wash in warm, soapy water. If this does not remove it, do not permit the piece to dry. Place stained area over a bowl, pour boiling water through the stain. Re-wash.

LIPSTICK   Try spot cleaning by rubbing petroleum jelly (such as Vaseline) into the spot. Then wash with warm, soapy water.

CANDLE WAX   Harden with an ice cube. Then flick the wax off with the reverse side (dull edge) of a knife. Place between two pieces of white paper towel. Press with a warm iron. Change paper frequently. Wash in warm, soapy water.

If colored wax still leaves a stain after removing the wax, try spot cleaning with alcohol. Then wash.

GREASE Spot cleaning with alcohol possibly will help. Then wash in warm, soapy water.

INK On white fabric, make a paste of salt and lemon juice. Rub into stain. Allow to set for at least two hours. Then wash in warm, soapy water.

On colored fabrics, soak stain in milk. Change milk often. Then wash in warm, soapy water. Hair spray will sometimes loosen ink stains. Then wash item.

WINE Apply table salt while stain is still wet. Let sit for two to four hours. Place stain over bowl and pour boiling water through it. If fabric is white, try spot cleaning with lemon juice and salt mixed to a paste. Finish by washing in warm, soapy water.

◆ THE FOLLOWING INFORMATION ON WASHING AND BLOCK-ING EMBROIDERY IS OF A *GENERAL* NATURE. It is strongly suggested that specific texts on the technique in question be consulted before washing or blocking is attempted.

◆ Washing of any embroidery should be done by hand. It is not appropriate to put needlework in a washing machine.

◆ If possible, use Orvus, which is a ph neutral soap, when washing embroidery. Many embroidery guilds have this soap for sale, and it can frequently be found in needlework shops. If it is not available, use a gentle soap rather than a detergent. Detergents tend to have chemicals in them which might cause problems. In addition, soap will usually rinse out easier, and more completely, than a detergent.

Dissolve soap in lukewarm water. A regular size sink usually provides sufficient room. If Orvus is being used, be certain not to use more than the amount which will coat one finger. Very little is required. When washing very large articles, increase amount accordingly. If a different soap is being used, start with a small amount, about one teaspoonful. Additional soap can be added if needed.

Needlework should be soaked no more than one or two minutes. 'Swish' gently to remove soil and grease. Do not wring or twist.

It is vitally important to completely rinse all soap from the embroidery. The rule of thumb is to continue rinsing until you are willing to drink the final water. If soap residue remains in the embroidery, it will attract dirt.

Roll needlework in a terry cloth towel to remove excess water. Squeeze gently. Do not wring or twist.

◆ After washing, embroidery such as canvas and crewel work should be blocked. Other items can be ironed dry.

◆ If ironing, use a dry iron and a pressing cloth. A terry towel should cover the ironing board. Place the embroidery on the towel, face down, and the pressing cloth on top of it. The pressing cloth can be any other piece of fabric, however washed, cotton muslin works especially well. Iron lightly. Do not allow the weight of the iron to remain in one position. Move iron vertically and horizontally, only. If the iron is moved on the diagonal, it tends to push the embroidery into a diagonal shape.

Iron lightly for a few minutes, then remove the pressing cloth. Keeping the needlework flat, permit it to air dry for ten to fifteen minutes. If allowed to air dry for too long, wrinkles will form. Iron again, being sure to use the pressing cloth. Repeat until ground fabric and threads are completely dry.

When ironing an embroidery, resist the urge to apply pressure to the fabric. Do not place iron directly on the needlework. Always use a pressing cloth.

♦ To bring washed needlework, such as crewel or needlepoint, back into straight alignment requires *blocking*. To block is to tack the work to a secure board, leaving it there until it is completely dry. Generally, crewel work should be routinely blocked after the embroidery is completed. As a basic rule, it is necessary to block that embroidery which you do not wish to be flattened by pressing with an iron.

♦ Manufactured blocking boards may be purchased at needlework shops. The directions that come with them should be followed carefully.

♦ A blocking board can be made of any material that will be firm enough to hold the work without shifting. It must also be soft enough that thumb tacks or staples can be put in it fairly easily. Consider making a board which is at least 24" x 24". This size will accommodate most needlework. A good blocking board can last about as long as you want to use it. It is wise to get, or make, it large enough to accommodate future designs of almost all sizes.

At one time it was popular to make blocking boards from plywood. However, it is very difficult to insert and remove staples from this wood. Also, chemicals and glue in plywood can easily leach into the embroidery causing premature rotting.

♦ Cellulose insulating fiber board makes an excellent blocking board. This is the material used for ceiling tile.

Insulating fiber board can be purchased at a building supply store. It usually comes in sheets that are 24" x 48". Most places are willing to sell a single sheet. It can be cut in half (24" x 24"), or to your require-

ments. The top side of the board is the one which appears to have a coat of ivory, or cream, paint.

The board should be covered with washed muslin to serve as a barrier between it and the embroidery. Wrap the muslin over the top of the board and secure on the reverse with staples. Make the fabric as tight as possible. Since blocked pieces must be accurately straightened, an alternative to the muslin covering is gingham with ½" squares. Be certain to wash it before covering the board. The squares of the gingham can serve as a line guide when positioning the pieces to be blocked.

◆　The piece to be blocked should be damp. If it has been washed, roll in a light colored terry cloth towel and gently squeeze out excess water. If the piece is dry, roll in wet towel and gently squeeze until damp. Place the piece on the covered board, face up. If it is blocked face down, the texture of the stitches will be flattened.

Using either a T-square or the print of the covering material as a guide, pull the embroidery into a rectangle or square. Make sure that sides are straight and perpendicular to each other. Place a staple or thumb tack at the center of one outside edge. Working alternately on either side of this staple, anchor the first side every ¼" to ½". Use the same procedure on an adjacent side. Then attach the two remaining sides with the same general method. Staples or tacks should be placed only near the edge of the ground material, well out of the design area.

Instead of beginning to staple in the center of one side, some find it easier to anchor each corner of the piece. Precede to insert staples on each side of the first four until the work is completely anchored.

It is necessary to exert a strong pull to bring the fabric into shape. The larger the piece, the greater muscles needed. You may want to enlist extra help when blocking large pieces.

◆ There is an alternate approach to blocking. It works well if the outside dimensions of the piece are known, or if the fabric is an irregular shape.

Cover the blocking board with paper. Draw a pencil outline to the finished dimensions. Place the damp needlework on top of the paper, pulling to fit the drawn pattern. Staple or thumb tack in place.

◆ Blocked pieces should be allowed to dry completely. This may take several days, depending on humidity in the area.

◆ Sometimes, after several hours of drying, ripples will appear on the surface of needlework being blocked. Simply remove the staples from two adjacent sides and re-tighten. Finish drying completely.

◆ Sometimes the tacks or staples used for blocking will leave rust spots. This is why it is important to place them at the very edge of the fabric. After the piece is dry, the rust spots can be cut off. If you leave rust on the material it possibly, in time, will cause holes in the fabric.

◆ If you have trouble understanding written directions, there are several things to try. First, read them through several times. Read the section completely. It is a mistake to read part of a section of instructions, then stop, do what they directed, then read more, do what that says, and so on. You must get an over-all understanding of the entire segment before you begin to stitch. Go through it two or three times, then pick up your needle.

◆ Should reviewing instructions not make them clear, try reading them into a tape recorder. Then play them back, all the way through, at least once, and even better, several times. Then play them again, this time stopping the tape after each direction. Follow the instructions of that portion, then go back to listening to the tape.

Alternating the hearing of the instructions and doing what they direct, after first listening to the entire section of instructions which pertain to a particular area, can almost always take care of the problem. It is possible that you are the type of person who learns better when hearing instructions rather than from written text.

◆　　If putting the directions on tape does not make them clear, consider going for help. Ask assistance from someone in your needlework chapter or guild, or from your local shop owner. If the directions were given in a class, contact the instructor for extra guidance.

◆　　If a chart, such as the commercial, copyrighted type used for counted cross stitch, is hard to understand, there are a couple of good solutions. Take the chart to the nearest copy machine and enlarge it. Not all copy machines will enlarge, so you might want to make a phone call before you head out. Almost all printers and private post offices have this service. The enlarged squares will be easier on your eyes and will make doing the stitches just that much simpler.

You might want to make a copy of the chart, enlarged or regular size, and color it. Use crayons or markers to color the chart with the colors of the threads to be used.

Be aware that you may copy the chart _only_ _for_ _your_ _own_ _use_. To copy a chart, and then give that copy to someone else, is against the law. It certainly is not pleasant to consider, but unfortunately several designers have been forced to bring suit against those who copy and share.

◆　　When you find it difficult to keep your place working a chart, try one of the magnetic line-minders available at needlework shops. They are excellent, and will make your life much easier. Some also magnify the line of stitches.

♦ Alternate methods of keeping your place include putting the points of your scissors at the spot on the chart where you are working, putting a ruler under the row you are stitching, coloring each symbol a different color, or checking off each stitch or row as you do them.

♦ When working on a dark ground fabric, it helps to put something white over your lap. The reverse is true if you are stitching a white or light ground. These contrasts are especially helpful when you need to count ground threads. The difference makes those threads easier to see.

♦ To change the size of a design before drawing it on your ground fabric, there are two basic methods.

Trace the design, even though it is the wrong size, on to tracing paper. Draw lines across it so that the tracing is divided into equal sized, small squares or rectangles.

On a second piece of paper, draw a frame the size of the desired design. Divide the frame into squares or rectangles. There must be the *same number of units* as there are on the first tracing of the design. In each unit, draw exactly what there is in the corresponding section on the original tracing. Then transfer this re-sized drawing to your ground fabric.

♦ Making drawings is an easy and inexpensive method to change the size of a prospective design. Unfortunately, it is generally time consuming.

An alternate method is to use a copy machine. While certainly more expensive, this approach is faster and more accurate.

Most copy machines will reduce or enlarge. Some machines have predetermined settings, some permit the user to decide the changes. Either way, experiment until the copy is the size you desire. Most print shops, office supply stores, or private post offices, which offer copy services, have adjustable copy machines. You probably will not find

such machines at a public library or drug store. Remember, if the design is not yours, copy only for your own use. To share copies of copyrighted work is illegal and unethical.

◆   Special care should be taken with designs which call for a section of dark wool stitches to be worked next to others in a light wool. Try to stitch the light values first. If the dark is worked first, then light wool stitches are stitched in the same fabric holes, or very close to each other, dark fibers will cling to those of the light wool. The transfer of dark fibers to light wool can cause the light to become muddied.

It is especially important to avoid stitching the dark value first when doing canvas work. In that case you may actually be working the light and dark wool in the same canvas holes.

Light/dark next to each other is less apt to cause a problem when stitching with smooth threads such as cotton or silk.

◆   If dark fibers have muddied stitches done in a light value, use a piece of white wool to help clean them. Cut about two inches of the white, and put it in a needle which is at least one size smaller than that used for the original stitches. Pull the needle, and the white wool, through the needle holes made for the light value stitches. The white will pick up the dark fibers clinging to the light value.

It may be necessary to clean the light value stitches more than once. Discard the used white wool and use a new piece each time.

Using white wool will help clean even smooth cotton or silk if it becomes muddied.

◆   Unfortunately, a needle can slip and you can get blood on your work. Natural chemicals such as a person's saliva will neutralize and remove that person's blood from most threads and many ground fabrics. Wet a length of white cotton thread with saliva and form into a ball. Dab the

blood stain. If the stain has soaked through to the back, be sure to treat the reverse, also. Repeat until no traces of blood can be seen. An extra precaution is to follow treatment by washing the complete article, if appropriate for fabric and thread. One person's saliva will not usually remove the blood of another person.

◆ Select items which offer the least color choice, first. For instance, if you want to do a design piece on colored canvas, you must decide on the canvas and the thread colors. The item with the least color choice is the canvas. Pick it first, then the threads that will go with that color. Or, if an item is to have a lining, think about selecting the lining first, then the threads. It is easier to choose from the rainbow of thread to match a selected lining fabric, or canvas, than the other way around.

◆ Generally, it is best not to have the mat on one side of a framed piece be one-half the size of the embroidery exposed in the mat opening. Thus, if the needlework showing inside the mat opening is 8″ x 8″, the mat should not be 4″ wide. With 4″ mat on each side of the needlework, the total mat is equal to the area of the embroidery. Have the mat cut either wider or narrower, depending on the effect you wish to convey.

As are most perceptions, this one is subject to personal opinion. However, it is the view of the majority of people.

◆ Another personal opinion, but one shared by many, is the position of the embroidery subject within a rectangular mat opening. The 'one-third at the bottom, two-thirds at the top' rule should always be considered.

For example, assume you have an embroidered flower with a background area. One-third of the background should visible between the lower edge of the object and the bottom mat. Two-thirds of the background should be between the top of the object and the top mat.

This positioning does have exceptions, such as when there is a stitched border around the central subject, or if the mat opening is square or round. However 'one-third, two-thirds' is something to think about when making decisions with your framer.

◆ Mat and frame colors will accentuate one or more colors in your piece. Before visiting the framer, consider which colors you want to emphasize.

◆ Be especially aware of the frame style and mat cut used for a wall hanging. A mat with elaborate cuts will draw attention away from the embroidery. The frame should enhance, not detract from the work. The needlework should be the focus of attention, not the mat or frame.

◆ Discuss mat and frame with your framer. Consider all his suggestions carefully. Then make a decision which will permit your needlework to be the focal point, not the work of the framer.

◆ If you are planning to enter a framed piece in an exhibit, and would like that piece under glass, consider taking an extra step. Have the framing done *without* glass. Enter the exhibit or competition. After the display, have the framer insert the glass. Most framers will do this for a very small, or no, extra charge. Exhibit judges can see the work better if it is not under glass. The better they can see your embroidery, the more apt you are to be rewarded with a ribbon.

◆ Avoid *non-glare* glass. The non-glare surface is created by an application of acid. The acid can cause a transfer of color and texture from the embroidery threads to the underside of the glass.

If, for whatever reason, you must have non-glare glass, be sure that there is a space between it and your embroidery. Hopefully there will be less reaction from the acid. Also note that non-glare glass, even if

placed directly on the needlework, causes the stitches to appear blurred.

♦ An interesting framing method is to mount the embroidery over a board which is covered in gold or silver lamé. Or, if you are not concerned about conservation, the piece could be mounted over a gold or silver board. Metallic mounting boards are generally not acid free, a condition which is important in conservation framing.

Mounting embroidery over a gold or silver backing, either fabric or board, allows the glint of the metallic to show through to the front. Such a twinkle can greatly enhance some needlework. If the ground fabric is an open weave, the metallic shows even better. Be careful that the metallic glints enhance, rather than detract from, the framed embroidery.

♦ The general principle of mounting over metallic can be expanded. Try mounting a piece, especially one with an open weave ground, over a colored board. This additional hint of color can improve the final presentation.

♦ Stretcher strips, or stretcher bars, make excellent working frames. However, working frames are questionable to use for a hanging display frame. They hold the fabric stretched, but provide no support in the middle. That nicely stretched fabric will soon start to sag when it is hung on a wall.

♦ The actual cost of the materials in a piece, the amount of time spent stitching it, and its value to you, determine to what extent you want to consider conservation. If all our needlework survives for 100 years, our descendants will be knee deep in embroidery. Some work is simply not intended to be around for that long. But those special pieces, the ones we want to pass on for generations, should be cared for with all the

preservation technology possible. This is true whether your piece is a framed wall hanging or intended for another use.

◆ Never display finished needlework in direct light or heat. Give completed pieces the same consideration you do your threads. Extensive exposure to light and heat cause rapid deterioration of embroidery whether it is under glass or not.

◆ If your finger is sore from the pressure of a needle, try using a rubber finger. You can find them in office supply stores.

◆ When you stitch several small dark sections in the middle of a light area, you can have lots of dark thread tails and nowhere to end them. Try collecting them together and tacking to the *back surface* of the work using the light thread. If you run them under the back of the lighter stitches, you will almost certainly form shadows which will show on the front. By anchoring on *top* of the back of the light stitches, the density of the light value stitches may cover the dark tails.

◆ When working on a project, stand back and look at it occasionally. Since we are so close to our work, we often loose the perspective of the whole design. Another suggestion is to place it on the back of a couch or on a mantle. Then leave the room for awhile. When you come back you will have a fresh viewpoint of the work.

◆ Because something is usually done a particular way does not mean that it is the only way. Be willing to experiment with your needlework.

◆ Congress cloth has a memory. If you put a needle into it in an area that is not later covered with stitching, you will leave a mark. To repair these needle holes, first gently put all canvas threads back into proper position with just the tip of a needle. Then, still using just the

tip of the needle, score the canvas both horizontally and vertically in the area of the mark. Do this by very gently dragging the needle's tip along the canvas channels. Be sure to do it *gently*. Take your time and repeat several times. This should help or eliminate your problem. The same solution frequently works well on larger mesh canvas.

◆ Your eyes can tire easily when doing needlework. Be sure to change your focus frequently. Take a few seconds to look up at something which is at a different distance than the stitching.

◆ It is important not to concentrate on your work for long periods of time. Limit intense work to an hour and a half, or two hours. Get up and move around. Stretch your arms, legs, and neck. Very sore muscles can result from stitching sessions which last too long without breaks. If necessary, set a timer to help you remember to take a break.

◆ Put your feet on a small stool to elevate them while you stitch. It helps circulation. Crossing your legs is bad for circulation. Make sure you have good lighting, but be careful of strong light such as direct sun. Too strong light will create a glare which hastens eye fatigue.

◆ Avoid storing needlework supplies anywhere that the humidity and temperature fluctuate radically. This includes places such as basements and attics.

ADDITIONAL THOUGHTS

Some personal observations from the author:

◆ When someone compliments you on your needlework, do not point out the mistakes, or where you could have done better. Just smile and say "thank you." Everyone knows that the next piece you do will be just that much better than the last one. We all advance in skill level as we practice. It is human nature to improve as we repeat actions. If you have spent your time on the work, you deserve the compliments. Accept them graciously.

◆ Perfection is unobtainable by mankind. However, by committing yourself to practice, excellence is well within reach. You can produce first rate work by doing it to the best of your ability. Capitalize on your strengths and stretch continually to improve your weaknesses. Everyone is capable of excellence in needlework.

◆ Most important of all, enjoy your needlework. If you do not enjoy the creative process, your time is wasted.